The Digital Divide

The Internet

ReferencePoint
Press®

San Diego, CA

Other books in the Compact Research The Internet set:

The Digital Divide

Peggy J. Parks

The Internet

ReferencePoint
Press®

San Diego, CA

© 2013 ReferencePoint Press, Inc.
Printed in the United States

For more information, contact:
ReferencePoint Press, Inc.
PO Box 27779
San Diego, CA 92198
www.ReferencePointPress.com

Picture credits:
© Kristian Buus/In Pictures/Corbis: 14
© Ed Kashi/Corbis: 12
Steve Zmina: 33–34, 47–49, 61–63, 75–76

LIBRARY OF CONGRESS CATALOGING-IN-PUBLICATION DATA

Parks, Peggy J., 1951–
    The digital divide / by Peggy J. Parks.
        p. cm. -- (Compact research)
    Includes bibliographical references and index.
    ISBN 978-1-60152-266-5 (hbk.) -- ISBN 1-60152-266-5 (hbk.)
 1. Digital divide--Juvenile literature. 2. Information society--Juvenile literature. I. Title.
    HM851.P362   2013
    303.48'33--dc23
                                                      2012021782

Contents

Foreword

66**Where is the knowledge we have lost in information?**99

—T.S. Eliot, "The Rock."

A s modern civilization continues to evolve, its ability to create, store, distribute, and access information expands exponentially. The explosion of information from all media continues to increase at a phenomenal rate. By 2020 some experts predict the worldwide information base will double every seventy-three days. While access to diverse sources of information and perspectives is paramount to any democratic society, information alone cannot help people gain knowledge and understanding. Information must be organized and presented clearly and succinctly in order to be understood. The challenge in the digital age becomes not the creation of information, but how best to sort, organize, enhance, and present information.

ReferencePoint Press developed the *Compact Research* series with this challenge of the information age in mind. More than any other subject area today, researching current issues can yield vast, diverse, and unqualified information that can be intimidating and overwhelming for even the most advanced and motivated researcher. The *Compact Research* series offers a compact, relevant, intelligent, and conveniently organized collection of information covering a variety of current topics ranging from illegal immigration and deforestation to diseases such as anorexia and meningitis.

The series focuses on three types of information: objective single-author narratives, opinion-based primary source quotations, and facts and statistics. The clearly written objective narratives provide context and reliable background information. Primary source quotes are carefully selected and cited, exposing the reader to differing points of view, and facts and statistics sections aid the reader in evaluating perspectives. Presenting these key types of information creates a richer, more balanced learning experience.

For better understanding and convenience, the series enhances information by organizing it into narrower topics and adding design features that make it easy for a reader to identify desired content. For example, in *Compact Research: Illegal Immigration*, a chapter covering the economic impact of illegal immigration has an objective narrative explaining the various ways the economy is impacted, a balanced section of numerous primary source quotes on the topic, followed by facts and full-color illustrations to encourage evaluation of contrasting perspectives.

The ancient Roman philosopher Lucius Annaeus Seneca wrote, "It is quality rather than quantity that matters." More than just a collection of content, the *Compact Research* series is simply committed to creating, finding, organizing, and presenting the most relevant and appropriate amount of information on a current topic in a user-friendly style that invites, intrigues, and fosters understanding.

The Digital Divide at a Glance

Digital Divide Defined

In general, the digital divide refers to the disparity between those who have access to high-speed Internet at home and those who do not.

Broadband

Broadband is defined by the Federal Communications Commission (FCC) as an Internet connection that can download data at speeds of at least 4 megabits (Mbps) per second and upload data at speeds of at least 1 Mbps.

Trends

Research by the National Telecommunications and Information Administration (NTIA) shows that 68 percent of US households had broadband as of 2011, compared with 51 percent in 2007.

The Least Access

The people with the least access to high-speed Internet are those with low incomes, those with low levels of education, residents of rural areas, people with disabilities, and minorities, especially Native Americans.

A Global Problem

Although the digital divide is a problem throughout the world, developing nations struggle far more than industrialized countries.

Causes

Contributing factors to the digital divide in the United States include little competition among Internet providers, poverty, and digital illiteracy.

Consequences

The lack of broadband access is especially problematic for job hunters, schools, and students.

Bridging the Gap

With billions of people worldwide unable to access high-speed Internet, governments are offering broadband subsidies for low-income people, expanding infrastructure, providing digital literacy training, and adopting other measures to help close the gap.

Overview

❝A deep digital divide—a chasm between those who have and have not yet adopted broadband—exists at a critical point in our nation's history where we are transitioning from an industrial to a digital society.❞

—David Honig, cofounder of the Minority Media and Telecommunications Council.

❝In the 21st century, having one-third of Americans sitting on the sidelines is as unthinkable as having one-third of our country without electricity in the 20th.❞

—Julius Genachowski, chair of the FCC.

The word *homework* has a different meaning for Eduardo Pérez than for many other students his age. Pérez, who is in the eighth grade at an Orlando, Florida, middle school, is often given assignments by his teachers that must be completed online. He is not able to work on the projects at home because his family cannot afford to buy a computer or to pay for Internet service. Although Pérez has a smartphone that he can sometimes use for research, staring at the tiny screen for long periods of time strains his eyes. So he depends on his mother to drive him to the library or to the home of a family member, where he can use a computer that is connected to the Internet. "It can be difficult for me," he says. "Sometimes I go to the school library before classes or try to do my homework and projects at school before coming home."[1]

Overview

What Is the Digital Divide?

Even in today's digital age, Pérez's situation is not uncommon. Tens of millions of people throughout the world struggle because they either cannot afford to pay for Internet service, live in areas where it is not available, or do not understand how to use a computer. As a result, the Internet's wealth of information is inaccessible to them. This disparity is known as the digital divide, which the public policy group Brookings Institution refers to as "the gap between society's tech-enabled haves and have-nots."[2]

According to the NTIA, an agency of the US Department of Commerce, the digital divide is widespread. In its February 2011 report *Digital Nation*, the NTIA states that nearly one-third of American households have no Internet connection. For many people this is a tremendous disadvantage because the medium is no longer merely a luxury or a "toy," as it was perceived in the past. Today the Internet is an essential tool for everything from conducting business to taking online classes, accessing health records, interacting with government agencies, and applying for jobs. Says the NTIA: "This resource can impact our nation's job base, productivity, competitiveness, economic growth, and ultimately, our standard of living. Given the high stakes, it matters that we are leaving some individuals behind."[3]

The Need for Speed

Most research on the digital divide focuses on broadband, which refers to high-speed Internet. Connection speeds are measured based on the number of bits (pieces of data converted to a digital format) that can be transferred from and to the Internet each second. The slowest connections, such as those that dial into the Internet using a telephone line, are measured in kilobits (1,000 bits) per second, or kbps, whereas broadband is measured in megabits (1 million bits) per second, or Mbps. According to the FCC, a broadband connection is one that can download (or downstream) data from the Internet to a user's computer at speeds of at least 4 Mbps and upload data from a user's computer to the Internet at speeds of at least 1 Mbps.

Speed is important because a fast-enough connection is essential for using many of the Internet's features—features that are inaccessible for people in rural areas where broadband is not available. While people with

A well-equipped technology training center provides students in eastern Washington with valuable computer and Internet experience. The Internet is an essential tool for communication, business, education, and employment in the twenty-first century.

a dial-up connection may have no problem sending and receiving e-mails, perusing simple web pages, or posting on Facebook, their connections are too slow for applications such as streaming video, videoconference services such as Skype, or watching movies. For example, it would take someone with a dial-up connection over twenty-nine hours to download a low-quality movie, whereas the same film would download in under an hour for someone with a broadband speed of 2 Mbps. Says James N. Barnes, who is an associate professor at Louisiana State University and director of the Louisiana Center for Rural Initiatives: "Suddenly, 'living in the land of dial-up' in rural America brings to light a significant reality: full participation in the knowledge economy is not possible with dial-up."[4]

Location and Income

Those who have broadband at home and depend on it every day may find it unbelievable that anyone still dials into the Internet. But for several million people in rural areas of the United States, dial-up service is the only option because broadband is not offered where they live. Availability differs from region to region, with some states having a much lower prevalence of broadband in rural areas than others. For instance, a June 2011 report by the FCC shows that 67 percent of the rural populations in New Mexico and Wyoming have no access to 3 Mbps broadband, compared with 5.5 percent of rural areas in Massachusetts and less than 10 percent in rural Pennsylvania and New Hampshire.

> **Today the Internet is an essential tool for everything from conducting business to taking online classes, accessing health records, interacting with government agencies, and applying for jobs.**

Along with the challenges posed by geographic location, income is a major factor in whether people have high-speed Internet connections at home. The NTIA *Digital Nation* report found that nearly 90 percent of US households with annual incomes of $150,000 and up have broadband, compared with 43 percent of households with incomes under $25,000. This disparity is even more pronounced when multiple factors are involved. For example, rural Hispanic-headed households with annual incomes under $25,000 have broadband adoption rates of only 30 percent.

Struggles of Tribal Areas

Of all those in the United States who are affected by the digital divide, none are more distanced from Internet technology than tribal populations. According to the FCC, there are 4.1 million American Indians and Alaska Natives in the United States and over 565 federally recognized tribes, with the Navajo and Cherokee being the two largest. Native Americans who live on tribal lands have some of the lowest rates of Internet use and accessibility in the United States. Over 90 percent lack high-speed Internet access, and usage rates are believed to be as low as 5 to 8 percent. In a March 2011 report, the FCC writes: "A deep digital divide persists between the Native Nations of the United States and the rest of the country."[5]

Young people in Kenya, some of whom have never seen a computer, learn to work with a basic word-processing program on a donated laptop. Parts of Kenya and other countries in the developing world have extremely limited access to computers and high-speed Internet.

A number of factors are responsible for the dearth of Internet availability among tribal populations, one of which is geographic location. Indian reservations tend to be located in remote, rugged areas that may not be connected to any road system, so installing the necessary infrastructure for broadband would be cost-prohibitive. Another reason Native Americans have such low Internet connectivity is income, as an extraordinarily high percentage live at or below the poverty level. Even if broadband were expanded to their areas, many could not afford to pay the monthly connection fee. The lack of broadband, says the FCC, is a serious problem for tribal populations, as it impedes their efforts "to preserve their cultures and build their internal structures for self-governance, economic opportunity, health, education, public safety, and welfare—in short, to secure a brighter future for their people."[6]

Unwired Nations

Many areas of the world have a digital divide problem, with the bleakest situation in developing countries such as India, Pakistan, Peru, and Brazil. According to a February 2011 report by the global research organization Euromonitor International, the countries with the least broadband access are found in Africa. In 2010, for instance, only 1.7 percent of households in Kenya had Internet service, and in Cameroon (a country about the size of California), the number of wired households was less than half that of Kenya.

Broadband use is growing rapidly in some developing countries, however. Statistics compiled by the International Telecommunications Union (ITU) show that the total number of fixed broadband users in developing nations rose more than 250 percent between 2005 and 2010, compared with industrialized countries that saw an average increase of just over 109 percent. Growth has been especially strong in China, where the number of broadband

> **Many areas of the world have a digital divide problem, with the bleakest situation in developing countries such as India, Pakistan, Peru, and Brazil.**

subscribers rose by 74.4 million between 2005 and 2010. The ITU writes: "Today, Internet users in China represent almost 25% of the world's total Internet users and 37% of the developing countries' Internet users."[7]

What Are the Causes of the Digital Divide?

Understanding the causes of the digital divide has been the focus of much research over the years. As far back as 1995, in its report *Falling Through the Net: A Survey of the "Have Nots" in Rural and Urban America*, the NTIA predicted that having access to the Internet would be an essential part of achieving success. The report stated: "While a standard telephone line can be an individual's pathway to the riches of the Information Age, a personal computer and modem are rapidly becoming the keys to the vault."[8] In that report, and in numerous studies conducted in the years since, the NTIA examines the correlation between Internet access in the home and income, education, race, and geographic location.

> As far back as 1995, in its report *Falling Through the Net: A Survey of the 'Have Nots' in Rural and Urban America*, the NTIA predicted that having access to the Internet would be an essential part of achieving success.

In terms of accessibility to broadband, a major contributor to the digital divide is that Internet service providers (ISPs) have complete control over which areas of the country will be served—and which will not. The extent of the region-to-region broadband disparity became clear in February 2011, when the NTIA published the first-ever nationwide map of broadband access in the United States. The map reveals information that was previously known only to ISPs, such as the specific types of Internet services (cable, fiber optic, DSL, and wireless) throughout the entire country, as well as the speed of the connections in each location.

One of the broadband map's most profound revelations was the close association between the wealth of an area and the presence of broadband. In Washington, DC, for instance, the poverty rate is 18 percent, and only 12 percent of homes have access to broadband speeds up to 25

Mbps. This is in sharp contrast to the wealthy DC suburb of Montgomery County, Maryland. With a poverty rate slightly over 5 percent, 98 percent of residents have access to 25 Mbps broadband.

Unhooked by Choice

Those who are most concerned about the digital divide consider it a "haves versus have-nots" issue, but in some cases the lack of Internet is not because of disadvantage—it is a personal choice. One finding of the NTIA *Digital Nation* study was that almost half (nearly 46 percent) of people without Internet access did not see any need to have it. This preference appears to be growing: In a report by the same group two years earlier, 37.8 percent of non-Internet users had indicated that they had no desire to have the service. Some experts attribute this to a lack of digital literacy, saying that people who are not online are unaware of how much the Internet can benefit their lives. Whatever the reason, it is a fact that millions of people have no interest in being connected to the Internet.

This is especially true among older people. Surveys show that compared with younger generations, only a fraction of senior citizens use the Internet. One of these surveys was published in August 2010 by the Pew Research Center's Internet & American Life Project. It found that only 31 percent of people over age 65 had broadband connections at home, compared with 80 percent of people aged 18 to 24 and 75 percent aged 30 to 49. Of non-Internet users aged 65 and over, most said they were not at all concerned about the lack of broadband access. Says Aaron Smith, Pew senior research specialist: "Seniors are significantly less likely than other age groups to view a lack of broadband access as a major disadvantage across a range of topics."[9]

> " In terms of accessibility to broadband, a major contributor to the digital divide is that Internet service providers (ISPs) have complete control over which areas of the country will be served—and which will not. "

What Are the Consequences of the Digital Divide?

For people who want broadband at home but cannot get it, the disadvantages are numerous. Children and teens may be able to use the Internet in school computer labs and libraries but have no way to complete online assignments at home. Businesses both large and small cannot operate effectively without high-speed Internet, yet broadband may not be available for those located in rural areas. Overall, conveniences that are widely taken for granted, such as e-mail, online shopping, Internet banking and bill paying, and keeping up with current news, are not accessible to those without broadband access. Says FCC chair Julius Genachowski:

> The costs of being shut out of our broadband economy are so high, and rising. More and more every day, not having broadband is a major barrier to finding and applying for a job, getting a world-class education, or obtaining access to health care. Today, lack of access to broadband is a much bigger obstacle to the opportunities that are essential for consumer welfare and America's economic growth and global competitiveness than it was even a few years ago.[10]

With his reference to education, Genachowski touched on one of the most worrisome problems associated with the digital divide. Although nearly all US schools have some sort of Internet connection in classrooms and/or computer labs, all kids do not benefit equally. Many are left behind because of stark differences from one school district to another, as educational consultant Lisa Gillis explains: "I've seen huge disparities, where I've gone into classrooms in urban districts and the paint is peeling and there's not a computer in sight, to very high-end districts where every kid has an iPad they can bring home. We have a long way to go."[11]

Tough Times for Job Hunters

The Internet has transformed how businesses find qualified employees. Human resources managers can post job openings on an organization's website and review the qualifications of applicants who post their resumes. According to the FCC, over 80 percent of Fortune 500 companies post jobs only on the Internet and will not accept applications unless they are submitted online. This saves time and money for employers but makes it difficult for job hunters who do not have broadband at home. Says Genachowski: "If you're not online—or if you're not digitally literate—the digital divide is now wider and deeper than ever before, hitting workers at all levels. Without home Internet, people are denied access to good jobs being created in America today."[12]

Jamal Mason knows from personal experience how tough it is to find a job in today's broadband-dominated work environment. Mason, who lives in New York City, had Internet service at home in the past but canceled it because the cost was too high. Now he takes the bus to the library every day to perform his job search, fill out online applications, and check his e-mail to see if any prospective employers have contacted him. Since patrons are only allowed forty-five minutes on the computers, he has to rush to get everything done, which he finds very discouraging. "I have to take a 20-minute bus from home just to get to the library," says Mason. "Then I come here and there's a time limit, so I'm racing the clock."[13]

> " Whatever the reason, it is a fact that millions of people have no interest in being connected to the Internet. "

Health-Care Barriers

Abundant information about health care is available on the Internet, from articles on every conceivable disease and disorder to important updates on medications and promising new treatments. According to a February 2011 report by the Pew Internet & American Life Project, searching online for health information is the third-most common online activity after checking e-mail and using a web search engine. In fact, says a 2011 American Medical Association article, "so much of health care is moving online that many physicians assume that everyone uses the Internet."[14] Everyone is not online, however, which means that a large segment of the population has no access to this information.

The same is true of patient health records, as a growing number of physicians are putting them online. As a result, people with Internet access can review laboratory test results and communicate by e-mail with

> " For many, tapping into this incredible resource is as simple as clicking a mouse—but not everyone has the ability to do that. "

health-care providers about a variety of issues. Says David W. Bates, who is internal medicine chief at Brigham and Women's Hospital in Boston: "There's already increasing evidence that using an online health record like this should improve the patient experience and quality of care. It's just very helpful to go and look at your lab tests at your leisure. And most providers believe that it's really to the patient's advantage to be more informed about the care they're getting." A study that Bates coauthored found that patients who are white, older, and/or wealthier are far more likely to benefit from this service. "The bottom-line," says Bates, "is that a digital divide does exist in terms of who tends to start using online personal health records."[15]

Can the Digital Divide Be Bridged?

Even though millions of people do not have high-speed Internet in their homes, research shows that this digital gap is slowly narrowing. According to the NTIA's *Digital Nation* report, broadband adoption among people with an annual income between $15,000 and $20,000 rose from 35 percent in 2009 to over 42 percent in 2010. Increases were also seen among all other income levels, age groups, and ethnicities.

Still, however, officials from the NTIA, FCC, and other agencies stress that much needs to be done to bridge the digital divide. According to Genachowski, this can happen only through shared commitments and people working together toward the same goal:

> Not surprisingly, our work has shown that there is no silver bullet to closing the adoption gap. No single program or actor alone—government, nonprofit, or private sector—can solve this national challenge. It will take all of the above, playing smart, mutually re-enforcing roles, acting boldly for both the near-term and long-term, and building on the increasing volume of best practices and data.[16]

Digital Dilemma

The Internet is becoming more crucial every day for education, job seeking, communication, health care, finding answers to innumerable questions, and keeping track of worldwide events. For many, tapping into this incredible resource is as simple as clicking a mouse—but not everyone has the ability to do that. With growing awareness of the digital divide, and expanding efforts to bridge it, the gap between the connected and the unconnected will likely continue to narrow in the coming years.

What Is the Digital Divide?

❝That is the cruel irony of the digital divide. With the Internet, we have this transformative technology that has the potential to level the playing field. But instead of equalizing opportunity, the Internet is actually increasing disparities because of the broadband adoption gap.❞

—David L. Cohen, executive vice president of Comcast Corporation.

❝As our jobs, entertainment, politics and even health care move online, millions are at risk of being left behind.❞

—Susan P. Crawford, professor at the Benjamin N. Cardozo School of Law and former White House special assistant for science, technology, and innovation policy.

The vast global network of networks that is now the Internet began as just two computers: one at the University of California–Los Angeles and the other 400 miles (644km) away at the Stanford Research Institute in Menlo Park, California. During an experiment in October 1969, the computers "talked" to each other across the miles, which marked the birth of what was then called ARPANET (Advanced Research Projects Agency Network). Word of the successful trial run began to spread, and as more computers were connected, the budding Internet grew rapidly. Over the next two decades, it was used primarily by scientists and technology gurus, as it was mysterious, complex, and difficult to navigate. Then British technology expert Tim Berners-Lee created the World Wide Web, which changed everything. Launched during the summer of 1991, the web opened the Internet to most anyone with a computer and modem—and sparked growth that was nothing short of phenomenal.

Small and large businesses developed websites and began using them to market their products and services, and government agencies started conducting business online using the web to interact with the public. Newspapers and magazines appeared online one by one, and virtual stores enticed people to do their shopping without ever having to leave their homes. As online communication and commerce continued to expand, technology experts began referring to the Internet as the "great equalizer," a medium that offered a wealth of opportunities that had never before been available. Yet while this progress was taking place, a small number of researchers began to notice a disturbing trend. Rather than serving as an equalizer, the Internet was slowly creating a chasm between segments of society that could access its information and those that could not. In the mid-1990s this gap was given a name: the digital divide.

Digital Divide Then and Now

Two researchers who had become concerned about the digital divide were James Katz, a social scientist at the technology company formerly known as Bellcore, and Philip Aspden, who was with the Center for Research on the Information Society. To evaluate whether the gap actually existed, they conducted one of the first demographic surveys on Internet use, and then published the results in a professional technology journal in 1997. In the article, Katz and Aspden shared their observation that cultural and racial inequalities existed online as they did in real life. Through the survey, they found that Internet users were generally wealthier and more educated than non-users, and that black and Hispanic people were "disproportionately unaware of the Internet." Having confirmed that the digital divide indeed existed, Katz and Aspden offered

> **Rather than serving as an equalizer, the Internet was slowly creating a chasm between segments of society that could access its information and those that could not.**

cautionary words about Internet use in the future: "To the extent that any demographic group becomes excluded from and underrepresented on the Internet, it will also be excluded from the economic fruits that such participation promises."[17]

Although Katz and Aspden wrote those words more than fifteen years ago, their depiction of the digital divide was much the same as the description used today—and research has shown that the Internet's exponential growth has deepened the divide. Studies conducted by the NTIA and the FCC have found that nearly two-thirds of people in the United States do not have high-speed Internet connections in their homes. A disproportionate number are lower-income families, those who are not highly educated, people with disabilities, minorities, and families who live in rural areas of the country.

> **The Internet was invented in the United States, but the United States lags behind many other industrialized countries in the number of people who are connected to it.**

These disparities were revealed in a survey published in April 2012 by the Pew Internet & American Life Project. Nearly 90 percent of participants with annual incomes over $75,000 had broadband at home, compared with 41 percent whose income was $30,000 per year or less. Pew researchers also found that Asian Americans and whites had the highest prevalence of home broadband connections, while blacks and Hispanics trailed behind. Distinct differences were also seen based on education levels. The survey showed that 85 percent of Americans with a college education had broadband at home, compared with only 22 percent of those without a high school diploma.

America Not a Broadband Leader

The Internet was invented in the United States, but the United States lags behind many other industrialized countries in the number of people who are connected to it. According to a June 2011 report by the Organisation for Economic Co-operation and Development, the top five global leaders for broadband subscriptions are Netherlands, Switzerland,

Denmark, South Korea, and Norway, with the next five being France, Iceland, the United Kingdom, Germany, and Sweden. Canada and three other countries also have greater broadband penetration than the United States, making its global ranking fifteenth place.

Along with connectivity, the United States also trails other industrialized countries in connection speed. For a 2012 report titled *The State of the Internet*, the global technology firm Akamai compiled worldwide broadband statistics and then ranked each country accordingly. With an average connection speed of 17.5 Mbps and a peak connection speed of 47.9 Mbps, South Korea was far ahead of the rest of the world. In Hong Kong and Japan, the average connection speed was 9.1 Mbps, tying them for second place in the global ranking. Next were Netherlands, Switzerland, Ireland, the Czech Republic, Romania, Belgium, Norway, and Finland, followed by the United States, whose average connection speed was 5.8 Mbps. "This is humiliating," says technology journalist John C. Dvorak, "but the U.S. has not even been in the top 10 for more than a decade."[18]

> " It is not only students in elementary through high school who struggle because of the digital divide—college students face hurdles as well. "

The Education Divide

The Internet is changing education in innumerable positive ways, from high-tech teaching methods used in classrooms to the extensive information students can find when doing research for assignments. According to a 2010 report by the National Center for Education statistics, 100 percent of public schools in the United States have at least one instructional computer with an Internet connection, and nearly all schools have them in classrooms. As promising as this is, however, many schools throughout the country are not able to meet students' technology needs. In its February 2011 report on broadband prevalence, the NTIA reports that two-thirds of American schools have Internet connections that are not fast enough for educational purposes.

Another problem is that vast disparities exist from one region to another, as well as between school districts in the same geographic area. One example is Bronzeville Scholastic Institute, a high school on the South Side of Chicago, where 93 percent of the 550 students are from low-income families. The twenty-four computers in the homework lab must be shared by nearly one thousand students from three different schools.

> Because of the exploding popularity of smartphones, wireless technology is radically changing the way people throughout the world connect to the Internet.

In stark contrast is the Deerfield Public School District, which is located 24 miles (38.62km) outside of Chicago. The high school, which was ranked seventh in the state of Illinois by *US News & World Report*, provides about two thousand computer workstations for thirty-one hundred students. Says Susan Patrick, president and CEO of the International Association for K-12 Online Learning: "Chicago in particular probably highlights the digital divide that's across the country."[19]

It is not only students in elementary through high school who struggle because of the digital divide—college students face hurdles as well. Those who live in rural areas where high-speed Internet is not available cannot take classes online because broadband is required. Also, many colleges require that applications, including those for federal financial aid, be filled out and submitted online. This caused frustration for Phelan Martin, a teenager who lives in an area of Vermont where broadband is not available and satellite service is too expensive for his family's budget. When he was applying to college, Martin had to fill out forms at his mother's office or at school, rather than at home. "It's been really tough to coordinate things," he says, "and I feel like it's put me at a disadvantage."[20]

Plight of the Disabled

One segment of society that is especially affected by the digital divide is people who have disabilities. According to a January 2011 survey by the Pew Internet & American Life Project, 54 percent of disabled adults use the Internet, compared with over 80 percent of those who do not have disabilities. Another finding of the survey was that when people with disabilities do use the Internet, they are less likely than other users to have broadband at home. For instance, 41 percent of disabled adults have home high-speed Internet, compared with 69 percent of people without disabilities. Says Susannah Fox, Pew's associate director for digital strategy: "Statistically speaking, disability is associated with being older, less educated, and living in a lower-income household. By contrast, Internet use is statistically associated with being younger, college-educated, and living in a higher-income household. Thus, it is not surprising that people living with disability report lower rates of Internet access than other adults."[21]

In June 2011 the World Health Organization released a publication called *World Report on Disability*. The report explains that being able to access the Internet enables people with disabilities to overcome potential physical, communication, and transportation barriers that they typically encounter offline. For instance, someone's disability may make it difficult to physically track down health-related information, whereas being able to search for it online simplifies the task. Those with hearing disabilities may feel more comfortable communicating online, where no one knows about their disability, rather than face-to-face. Also, because people with disabilities often feel isolated and alone, the ability to interact with others on the Internet (such as in online forums) can make them feel included, like they are members of a community. The authors of the World Health Organization report write: "People with disabilities, once they are able to access the web, value the health information and other services provided by it."[22]

Wired Versus Wireless

Because of the exploding popularity of smartphones, wireless technology is radically changing the way people throughout the world connect to the Internet. In fact, studies have shown that smartphones are growing at three times the rate of personal computers, and mobile broadband subscriptions have surpassed those of fixed broadband. A survey by the Pew Internet & American Life project found that between May 2011 and February 2012, smartphone ownership among people with annual incomes of $30,000 or less increased more than for all other income levels, and growth has also been strong among minorities. Says Darrell M.

West, who is founding director of the Brookings Institution's Center for Technology Innovation: "For the first time, people are able to reach the Internet in a relatively inexpensive and convenient manner. Regardless of geographic location, they can use mobile broadband for communications, education, health care, public safety, disaster preparedness, and economic development."[23]

Yet not everyone is enthusiastic about the growing preference for wireless mobile Internet connections. Susan P. Crawford, who is a law professor and former White House special assistant for science, technology, and innovation policy, says it is not surprising that smartphones are growing in popularity among low-income people and minorities, because the monthly cost is about half as much as wired broadband. Her perspective, however, is that smartphone Internet access "is not a substitute for wired."[24]

Even though smartphones do provide Internet access, often for many who could not afford it before, Crawford says that users are hampered by slow connections and limits on the amount of data that can be transferred. If they exceed the allotted amount, overage charges are tacked on by the provider. For these and other reasons, she is convinced that mobile technology has not actually helped people overcome the limitations of the digital divide. She writes: "While we still talk about 'the' Internet, we increasingly have two separate access marketplaces: high-speed wired and second-class wireless. High-speed access is a superhighway for those who can afford it, while racial minorities and poorer and rural Americans must make do with a bike path."[25]

The Gap Persists

The digital divide is a global problem that began to emerge within a few years of the launch of the World Wide Web. The technology have-nots, as they are often called, include people who live in rural areas, those with low income and little education, minorities, and people with disabilities. Although mobile technology has increased people's ability to connect to the Internet, the gap between people who have ready access to broadband and those who do not still exists—and research shows that it has continued to widen. Says the FCC's Julius Genachowski: "The digital divide is more troubling than ever because the costs of digital exclusion are rising."[26]

Primary Source Quotes*

What Is the Digital Divide?

66 Racial and ethnic differences in computer use and Internet access have long existed, and while progress has been made, over the past decade in narrowing these gaps, disparities still exist. 99

—Kaiser Family Foundation, "The Digital Divide and Access to Health Information Online," Kaiser Public Opinion, April 2011. www.kff.org.

The Kaiser Family Foundation specializes in health policy analysis, health journalism, and communication.

66 In the 1990s, there was a horrendous, general caterwauling about the 'digital divide.' How can we move together as a society without getting poor minorities on the Internet as quickly as possible? They need to download porn, too! Will the have-nots be left out of the Web revolution? It was a really, really, silly debate. 99

—Jonah Goldberg, "Proof of Life," *Daily*, March 18, 2012. www.thedaily.com.

Goldberg is editor at large of *National Review Online* and a fellow at the American Enterprise Institute.

Primary Source Quotes

"The concept of the digital divide has been evolving over the years, being generally defined as a social issue linked to the different amount of information between those individuals who have access to the information society and information and communication technology and those who do not."

—Andreea Stoiciu, "The Role of E-governance in Bridging the Digital Divide," *UN Chronicle*, September 2011. www.un.org.

Stoiciu is the executive director of the Institute for Management and Sustainable Development in Romania.

"Were broadband truly available to all unserved Americans, we would expect to see greater adoption than we see today given how vital broadband has become to so many aspects of economic and social life."

—National Telecommunications and Information Administration, *Digital Nation: Expanding Internet Usage*, February 2011. www.ntia.doc.gov.

An agency of the Commerce Department, the NTIA is responsible for advising the president on telecommunications and information policy issues.

"Persistent gaps between developed and developing nations, as well as gaps domestically along socioeconomic, geographic, educational, racial, and gender lines, have broadly come to be known as the 'digital divide'—a term that both names these disparities and stands as a marker for the concerns about them."

—Dmitry Epstein, Erik C. Nisbet, and Tarleton Gillespie, "Who's Responsible for the Digital Divide? Public Perceptions and Policy Implications," *Information Society*, March 4, 2011. www.sri.cornell.edu.

Epstein and Gillespie are with Cornell University's Department of Communication, and Nisbet is with Ohio State University's School of Communication.

66 **The digital divide is real: not every student has reliable access to the Internet, particularly those in rural areas where even public libraries are a luxury.** 99

—Stephanie Rosalia, "Students Should Not Abandon Print," *Room for Debate* (blog), *New York Times*, March 15, 2012. www.nytimes.com.

Rosalia is a school librarian in New York City.

66 **There has been good progress, yet almost one-third of American households still lack a broadband connection. We need to make sure no one is left behind in the digital age.** 99

—Lawrence E. Strickling, foreword to *Digital Nation: Expanding Internet Usage*, National Telecommunications and Information Administration, February 2011. www.ntia.doc.gov.

Strickling is assistant secretary for communications and information at the Commerce Department.

66 **Broadband has quickly become an essential service that plays a key role in creating and keeping jobs in rural America.** 99

—Mark Bahnson, "Formulation of the 2012 Farm Bill: Rural Development Programs," testimony, House Committee on Agriculture, April 25, 2012. http://agriculture.house.gov.

Bahnson is CEO and general manager of Bloomingdale Communications in Bloomingdale, Michigan.

66 **It took digital-divide researchers a whole decade to figure out that the real issue is not so much about access to digital technology but about the benefits *derived from access*.** 99

—Craig Warren Smith, "'Digital Divide' Defined (Hint: It's Not About Access)," Digital Divide Institute, May 7, 2012. www.digitaldivide.org.

Smith is the founder of the Digital Divide Institute.

Facts and Illustrations

What Is the Digital Divide?

- According to the Freedom Rings Partnership, Philadelphia has one of the widest digital divides in the United States, with **41 percent** of residents having no access to a computer or the Internet.

- A February 2011 report by the NTIA states that **68 percent** of US households have broadband, which is an increase over 2007, when this was the case with **51 percent** of households.

- A 2012 study by the global technology firm Akamai found that the number one city in the world for broadband connection speed is **Taegu, South Korea**.

- According to the Information Policy & Access Center, the number of US libraries that offer Internet access has jumped from under **13 percent** in 1994 to **99 percent** in 2012.

- According to a February 2011 report by Euromonitor International, the number of Internet users worldwide totaled **2 billion** in 2010, which is double the 1 billion reported in 2005.

- A January 2011 survey by the Pew Internet & American Life Project found **41 percent** of adults living with a disability have broadband Internet at home, compared with **69 percent** of nondisabled adults.

Countries at Opposite Ends of Digital Divide

To get the most out of the Internet's information-rich content, merely being connected is not enough. Without a fast connection speed, Internet users cannot make use of online class lectures, streaming video, movies, or music. Countries with high-speed Internet connections are seen to be on the winning side of the digital divide while countries that lack these connections are at risk of being left behind.

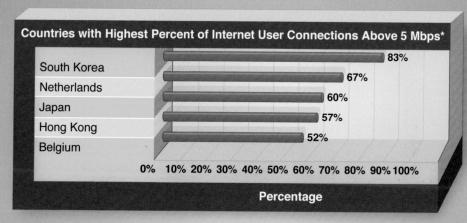

Countries with Highest Percent of Internet User Connections Above 5 Mbps*

Country	Percentage
South Korea	83%
Netherlands	67%
Japan	60%
Hong Kong	57%
Belgium	52%

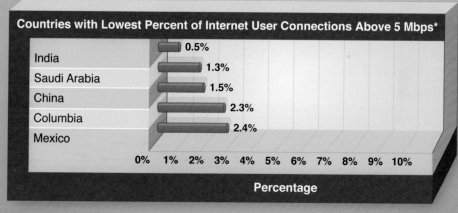

Countries with Lowest Percent of Internet User Connections Above 5 Mbps*

Country	Percentage
India	0.5%
Saudi Arabia	1.3%
China	1.5%
Columbia	2.3%
Mexico	2.4%

Note: *Internet speeds are measured in kilobits (kbps) or megabits (Mbps), which refer to the amount of data transferred per second; 1 Mbps is equivalent to 1 million bits per second or 1,000 kbps.

Source: Akamai, *The State of the Internet: 4th Quarter, 2011 Report*, 2012. www.akamai.com.

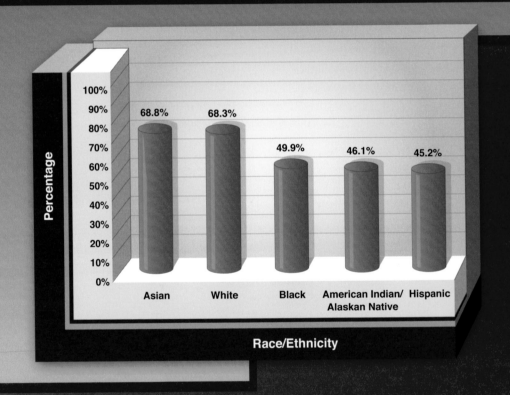

Home Broadband Highest Among Asians, Whites

Studies that focus on high-speed, or broadband, Internet connections in US households clearly show disparities among demographic groups. As this graph illustrates, Hispanics had the lowest prevalence of broadband in the home during 2009 and 2010, followed by American Indians/Alaskan Natives.

Percent of Households with Broadband by Race and Ethnicity, 2010

Asian: 68.8%
White: 68.3%
Black: 49.9%
American Indian/Alaskan Native: 46.1%
Hispanic: 45.2%

Source: US Department of Commerce: National Telecommunications and Information Administration, *Digital Nation: Expanding Internet Usage*, February 2011. www.ntia.gov.

- According to **Vermont** governor Peter Shumlin, in terms of high-speed Internet connectivity, his state ranks behind China, Vietnam, Bosnia, and Croatia.

- A 2012 study by the global technology firm Akamai found that the North African country of Morocco rose from having broadband in **2 percent** of homes in 2004 to **25 percent** in 2011.

- According to the FCC, the states of **Utah, New Hampshire, and Washington** have the highest rates of US broadband adoption, while **Mississippi, Arkansas, and Alabama** have the lowest rates.

- According to an October 2011 report by the International Telecommunications Union, in developing countries **30 percent** of people under age 25 use the Internet, compared with **23 percent** of those aged 25 and older.

- A 2010 report by the FCC found that **39 percent** of American adults who do not have broadband access are living with a disability.

- According to a 2011 report by the NTIA, **two-thirds** of US schools surveyed have a broadband connection lower than **25 megabits** per second.

- As of 2012 three US states (Alabama, Florida, and Michigan) required that students complete at least **one online** class before graduating from high school, and Idaho's requirement was **two online** classes.

What Are the Causes of the Digital Divide?

66Getting a high speed Internet connection in the US costs consumers more money than it does in other countries, so less people can afford it.99

—David Belson, director of market intelligence for the global technology firm Akamai.

66While the numbers of new broadband subscribers continue to grow, studies and data suggest that the rate of broadband deployment in urban/suburban and high income areas are outpacing deployment in rural and low-income areas.99

—Lennard G. Kruger, a specialist in science and technology policy, and Angele A. Gilroy, a specialist in telecommunications policy.

In March 2002 the FCC made a decision that profoundly changed the nature of broadband Internet service in the United States. To settle an ongoing debate over the regulatory classification of high-speed Internet, the agency declared it to be an "information service" rather than a "telecommunications service." Unlike telephone companies, which were legally required to lease their lines to competing service providers, broadband providers were exempt from this regulation. The ruling gave ISPs complete control over their infrastructures, meaning that they could decide for themselves whether or not to lease to competing broadband providers. In a news release announcing its decision, the FCC explained that the reclassification would "encourage the ubiquitous availability of broadband access to the Internet to all Americans" and "ensure that broadband services exist in a minimal regulatory environment that promotes investment and innovation."[27]

A Decade of Progress and Decline

The measure adopted by the FCC did indeed lead to "investment and innovation." In the years since the ruling went into effect, broadband providers have spent tens of billions of dollars expanding their networks throughout the country. In turn, broadband adoption among American households has soared from just 4.4 percent in 2000 to over 68 percent in 2010. But other developments over that period of time have not been positive, including the United States' decline in the global broadband ranking. According to reports by the Organisation for Economic Co-operation and Development, which compiles statistics and makes policy recommendations to member nations, the United States was ranked fourth in the world in 2001 for household broadband subscribers—and by 2011 it had dropped to fifteenth place.

Also in the years since the FCC's ruling, the digital divide has steadily widened. A 2000 report by the NTIA noted that broadband adoption in rural versus urban households differed by 5 percentage points, whereas the agency's 2011 *Digital Nation* report said the gap had doubled to 10 percentage points. Even more profound was the change in disparity based on household income. The NTIA's 2000 report showed that 7.7 percent of households with annual income below $15,000 had broadband, compared with 13.8 percent of households with income over $75,000; a

> " According to reports by the Organisation for Economic Co-operation and Development . . . the United States was ranked fourth in the world in 2001 for household broadband subscribers—and by 2011 it had dropped to fifteenth place. "

difference of 6.1 percentage points. According to the 2011 report, 32 percent of low-income households had broadband, compared with 85.5 percent of those over $75,000 per year—a difference of 50 percentage points.

Although no one can say with any certainty whether the FCC's decision caused the worsening of America's digital divide, many are convinced that it did. An October 2010 editorial in *Scientific American* clearly pins the blame on the ruling, referring to broadband service in the United States as "awful" and calling the FCC's reclassification of broadband service "a terrible mistake." The editors contend that since the country's handful of large broadband providers are not subject to government regulation, they have a monopoly over broadband service, and customers pay the price for that—literally and figuratively. "In practice," the editors write, "it has stifled competition."[28]

> With relatively few companies controlling access to high-speed Internet in the United States, competition is minimal—and many claim that consumers suffer as a result.

According to New Jersey resident Tom Smith, the *Scientific American* editorial and its claim about the stifling of competition are "right on the money."[29] Although he lives in a large, densely populated city, Smith still has only two choices for Internet service: the telephone company or the cable company. Both ISPs provide connection speeds that are only about one-fourth of the FCC's 4 Mbps benchmark for high-speed Internet, yet both charge $50 per month for their service. Smith finds this exceedingly frustrating and blames the problem on the 2002 reclassification, as he writes: "The FCC let the big companies have their way and they have given us some of the worst Internet and telephone service in the world."[30]

Little Competition

With relatively few companies controlling access to high-speed Internet in the United States, competition is minimal—and many claim that consumers suffer as a result. As Smith's situation indicates, the dearth of competition among ISPs means that people who want broadband in their homes have no choice but to take whatever services are available. This puts them at a disadvantage since they are prevented from shopping around to find the best prices and service. Says Susan P. Crawford: "Lacking competition from other cable companies or alternate delivery technologies, each of the country's large cable distributors has the ability to raise prices in its region for high-speed Internet services. Those who can still afford it are paying higher and higher rates for the same quality of service."[31]

The relationship between low competition and pricing set by broadband providers was one of the focuses of a study published in February 2010 by Harvard University's Berkman Center for Internet & Society. The report describes how the prices consumers pay for high-speed Internet are directly proportional to the number of providers who offer service in a particular area. Based on reports from broadband subscribers, the Berkman team learned that when four or more ISPs are operating in a particular area, the monthly cost is $32.10. When the number of providers is reduced to three, the price goes up to $38.10 and rises to $42.80 when only two providers are available.

The report goes on to state that when a market is dominated by only one broadband provider, the price increases to $44.70—nearly 140 percent of the cost found in areas where broadband services are most competitive because of multiple providers. Although the Berkman report makes it clear that factors other than competition may come into play with these price differences, the authors say it would be "equally speculative" to assume that the lack of competition plays no role in the prices that ISPs charge. They write: "The difference is likely a combined effect of cost and lack of competition that varies by location."[32]

Less for More

In the same way that US broadband prices and connection speeds vary widely from region to region, they also differ from those of other countries—and studies have consistently shown that Americans pay higher prices for slower connections. This was a major finding of an April 2010 report by New America Foundation's Open Technology Institute, which focused on worldwide connection speeds and broadband costs. The United States did not fare well in the study, as the report authors write:

"In comparing prices and speeds of broadband services around the globe, we find that the United States is among the most expensive and slowest of the countries surveyed in this report. Price is one of the main barriers to adoption, and prices for broadband in the U.S. are on the rise."[33]

> " In March 2012 the Investigative Reporting Workshop published a study that examined Internet access in all fifty US states and found a close association between broadband availability and wealth. "

The researchers who performed the Open Technology Institute study analyzed connection speed based on tiers, meaning low- versus high-speed broadband connections, and then performed calculations to arrive at a per-megabit price. When examining low-tier service (1 through 10 Mbps) in ten countries, the team found that the United Kingdom had the lowest cost at $3.00 per megabit, closely followed by South Korea at $3.25 per megabit. At $35 per megabit for low-tier connections, the United States was by far the costliest of all countries studied.

The price comparison was even more striking when the researchers examined high-tier broadband service. At just 29 cents per megabit in South Korea and 30 cents per megabit in Japan, these countries were clearly the worldwide value leaders. In stark contrast was the United States, whose cost per megabit was $2.90. To put this in perspective, customers in South Korea pay $29 per month for 100 Mbps, whereas people in the United States pay $145 for a connection speed that is only half as fast. As the *Scientific American* editors write: "The average U.S. household has to pay an exorbitant amount of money for an Internet connection that the rest of the world would find mediocre."[34]

Poverty Is a Factor

Numerous reports by government agencies and independent research groups have shown that geographic location plays a major role in who has access to broadband and who does not. This is true not only in the United States, but also in other countries. In general, remote, rural areas are much less likely to have broadband access than highly populated urban regions. Says John Dunbar, who is managing editor for politics and finance at the Center for Public Integrity: "Rural areas have historically suffered from lower broadband subscription rates. There's less money to be made with lower population densities, and it costs more to run wires to those areas."[35]

In March 2012 the Investigative Reporting Workshop published a study that examined Internet access in all fifty US states and found a close association between broadband availability and wealth. The study involved collecting comprehensive broadband data from the FCC, as well as demographic information (such as income, race, and age) from the US Census Bureau. By analyzing this data, researchers could see that wealthier states such as Connecticut, New Jersey, Massachusetts, and New Hampshire had

> "As research continues, experts will undoubtedly learn more about why these disparities exist, which can help government agencies and policy makers figure out how to best address the problem."

the country's highest broadband subscription rates. In stark contrast were the southern states of Mississippi, Arkansas, Alabama, Tennessee, and West Virginia, all of which have exceptionally high rates of poverty and what Dunbar calls "abysmal"[36] broadband subscription rates.

Of the entire country, the metropolitan area with the highest poverty rate is McAllen, Texas, which is located 5 miles (8.05km) from the Mexican border in Hidalgo County—and the Investigative Reporting Workshop study found that it has the lowest broadband subscription rate in the United States. Jose A. Gamez, who is director of McAllen's public libraries, says that this finding does not surprise him. "Hidalgo County is one of the poorest counties in the country," he says, "so a lot of people here just can't afford their own computers or the broadband connection."[37]

In the Dark

Most publicity about the digital divide focuses on causes such as the inability to afford broadband at home and low availability in rural areas of the country. Studies have shown, however, that people who do not have home broadband often think that a higher-speed connection is unnecessary or are not interested in the Internet at all. According to John B. Horrigan, who is vice president of policy research at the technology industry firm TechNet, these nonusers question the Internet's relevance to their lives. "They do not believe digital content is sufficiently compelling to justify getting it," says Horrigan. "Specifically, these non-adopters say the Internet is a 'waste of time,' do not think there is anything worth seeing online and (for dial-up users) say they are content with their current service."[38]

The NTIA's *Digital Nation* report confirmed Horrigan's observation: When asked the main reason for not having a household broadband connection, over 46 percent of respondents said they did not need it or were not interested. When people using dial-up connections were asked the same question, one-third said broadband was too expensive, and nearly the same number said that broadband did not interest them. Many are convinced that this sums up the situation in rural America: People who dial in to the Internet often cannot afford to pay for faster connections, and even if affordability is not an issue, they are not aware of the advantages offered by broadband. According to Edyael Casaperalta, who is with the Center for Rural Strategies in Whitesburg, Kentucky, the notion that people in rural areas do not care about the Internet is an inaccurate stereotype. Rather, she says, people seemingly lack interest because they do not fully understand the Internet and have no idea how much it can benefit them. Speaking metaphorically, Casaperalta says: "We're getting blamed for not liking books when we haven't been taught to read."[39]

A Combination of Causes

A number of contributing factors have been identified as causes of the digital divide. These include the deregulation of ISPs, lack of competition among providers, low awareness of the benefits of high-speed Internet, low income, and geographic location. As research continues, experts will undoubtedly learn more about why these disparities exist, which can help government agencies and policy makers figure out how to best address the problem.

Primary Source Quotes*

What Are the Causes of the Digital Divide?

66 So America, the country that invented the Internet and still leads the world in telecommunications innovation, is lagging far behind in actual use of that technology. The answer to this puzzle is regulatory policy. 99

—Susan P. Crawford, "The New Digital Divide," *New York Times*, December 3, 2011. www.nytimes.com.

Crawford is a professor at the Benjamin N. Cardozo School of Law and a former White House special assistant for science, technology, and innovation policy.

66 History and evidence suggest that deregulation is what has given us one of the best broadband marketplaces in the world. 99

—John Stephenson, "Central Planning Won't Close the 'New Digital Divide,'" *Heartlander*, February 29, 2012. http://news.heartland.org.

Stephenson is the director of the Communications and Technology Task Force at the American Legislative Exchange Council.

Bracketed quotes indicate conflicting positions.

* Editor's Note: While the definition of a primary source can be narrowly or broadly defined, for the purposes of Compact Research, a primary source consists of: 1) results of original research presented by an organization or researcher; 2) eyewitness accounts of events, personal experience, or work experience; 3) first-person editorials offering pundits' opinions; 4) government officials presenting political plans and/or policies; 5) representatives of organizations presenting testimony or policy.

❝Addressing the reasons for—and the solutions to—the 'digital divide' has been on the public agenda since the emergence of the Internet.❞

—Dmitry Epstein, Erik C. Nisbet, and Tarleton Gillespie, "Who's Responsible for the Digital Divide? Public Perceptions and Policy Implications," *Information Society*, March 4, 2011. www.sri.cornell.edu.

Epstein and Gillespie are with Cornell University's Department of Communication, and Nisbet is with Ohio State University's School of Communication.

❝Education is a particularly strong predictor of broadband use.❞

—National Telecommunications and Information Administration, *Digital Nation: Expanding Internet Usage*, February 2011. www.ntia.doc.gov.

An agency of the Commerce Department, the NTIA is responsible for advising the president on telecommunications and information policy issues.

❝India's Internet penetration has been low due to a lack of affordability—as well as infrastructure—for connectivity.❞

—Suneet Singh Tuli, "Bridging the Digital Divide," *Management Compass*, January 2012. www.mediamates.biz.

Tuli is the founder and CEO of the web access provider DataWind.

❝The vast distance and sparse populations make the costs of building broadband-capable networks in rural areas quite high.❞

—Mark Bahnson, "Formulation of the 2012 Farm Bill: Rural Development Programs," testimony, House Committee on Agriculture, April 25, 2012. http://agriculture.house.gov.

Bahnson is CEO and general manager of Bloomingdale Communications in Bloomingdale, Michigan.

66 Every major survey has shown that the lower the income, the less likely it is that households will subscribe to the Internet. 99

—John Dunbar, "Poverty Stretches the Digital Divide," *Investigative Reporting Workshop*, March 23, 2011. http://investigativereportingworkshop.org.

Dunbar is managing editor for politics and finance at the Center for Public Integrity.

66 Many . . . Americans live in areas where there is no business case to offer broadband, and where existing public efforts to extend broadband are unlikely to reach; they have no immediate prospect of being served, despite the growing costs of digital exclusion. 99

—Federal Communications Commission, "Seventh Broadband Progress Report and Order on Reconsideration," May 20, 2011. http://transition.fcc.gov.

The FCC is an independent US government agency that is charged with regulating interstate and international communications by radio, television, wire, satellite, and cable.

66 To take full advantage of the economic opportunities enabled by broadband . . . more Americans need online skills. For instance, broadband service allows a small business owner in rural America to sell her goods to consumers around the world—but online skills are also required. 99

—Anna M. Gomez, "Digital Literacy Is Part of Job Preparedness," *The White House Blog*, White House, August 29, 2011. www.whitehouse.gov.

Gomez is deputy assistant secretary for communications and information and deputy administrator of the NTIA.

What Are the Causes of the Digital Divide?

- According to a 2011 report by the NTIA, the two most common reasons given for having no home broadband are that it is not needed **(46 percent)** and is too expensive **(25 percent)**.

- According to an April 2010 report by the New America Foundation, in terms of lower-speed broadband, the **cost per megabit** in the United Kingdom is **$3.00**, in South Korea **$3.25**, and in the United States **$35.00**.

- A 2010 FCC survey found that **93 percent** of households with annual income over $75,000 had broadband Internet service, compared with **40 percent** of households with income below $20,000.

- A study published in March 2012 by the Investigative Reporting Workshop found that the US state with the lowest home broadband subscribership rate was **Mississippi**, which is also the poorest state in the country.

- Euromonitor International reports that due to more advanced infrastructure, higher government spending on technology, and large incomes, nearly **98 percent** of South Korean households had broadband Internet service in 2010, compared with **1.7 percent** in Kenya and **1.3 percent** in Pakistan.

Broadband Use Increases with Income

Studies by government agencies and research organizations continue to show a connection between income levels and the prevalence of broadband in the home, as many low-income people cannot afford the service. A study published in April 2012 by Pew Research Center's Internet & American Life Project found that only 41 percent of households with annual income under $30,000 had home broadband compared with 89 percent of households with annual income over $75,000.

Percent of households with broadband access by yearly income

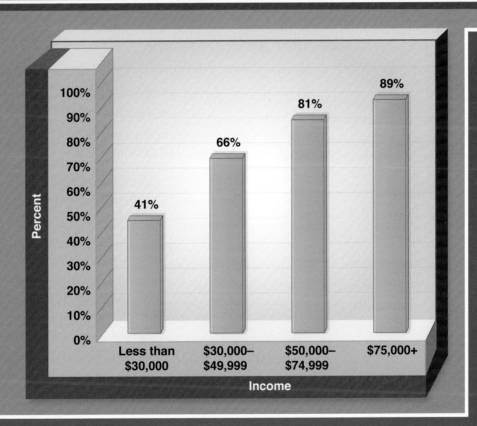

Source: Pew Research Center's Internet & American Life Project, *Digital Differences*, April 13, 2012. http://pewinternet.org.

- A January 2011 survey by the Pew Internet & American Life Project found that **2 percent** of American adults have a disability or illness that makes it harder or impossible to use the Internet.

Broadband Costly in United States

Studies by government agencies and independent research groups have shown that many countries of the world have a much greater prevalence of home broadband (high-speed) Internet than the United States. One factor is cost. According to a December 2011 report by the Canadian research consulting firm Lemay-Yates Associates, the United States ranks fifteenth in terms of monthly cost for broadband over 10 Mbps*.

Broadband Service Average Monthly Cost in US Dollars

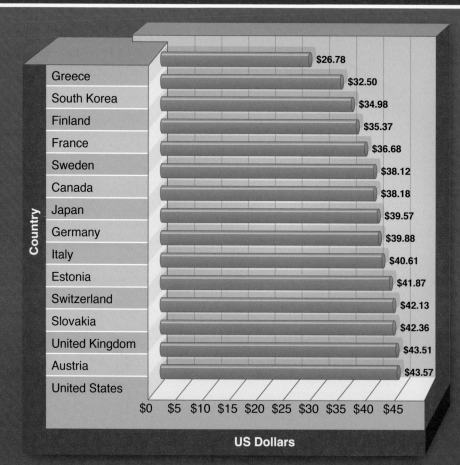

*The fastest Internet speeds are measured in megabits (Mbps), which refer to the amount of data transferred per second; 1 Mbps is equivalent to 1 million bits per second.

Source: Lemay-Yates Associates, "Comparative Assessment of Broadband Performance and Cost for Consumers in G7 and OECD Countries," December 2011. www.lya.com.

Disinterest in the Internet

Researchers cite many reasons for the digital divide. Some, such as low income level, are frequently beyond the individual's control. One cause, however, is entirely a matter of personal choice. A 2012 Pew Research Center project found that 31 percent of people without Internet or e-mail access are simply not interested in using either of these online tools.

What is the MAIN reason you don't use the Internet or email?

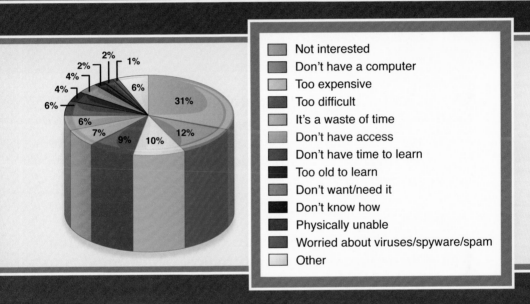

Legend:
- Not interested
- Don't have a computer
- Too expensive
- Too difficult
- It's a waste of time
- Don't have access
- Don't have time to learn
- Too old to learn
- Don't want/need it
- Don't know how
- Physically unable
- Worried about viruses/spyware/spam
- Other

Source: Pew Center's Internet & American Life Projects *Digital Difference*, April 13, 2012. http://pewinternet.org.

- According to a 2011 report by the NTIA, **57 percent** of rural households have access to broadband Internet service, compared with **70 percent** of urban households.

- In a March 2010 survey by the FCC, **22 percent** of respondents said they did not use the Internet because they were not comfortable with computers and/or were worried about bad things that could happen online.

What Are the Consequences of the Digital Divide?

66 The lack of a broadband connection puts people at a profound disadvantage. People without access, who are likely to be lower on the economic ladder, fall further and further behind, widening the 'digital divide' between rich and poor. 99

—John Dunbar, managing editor for politics and finance at the Center for Public Integrity.

66 The costs of digital exclusion are high and growing: lack of broadband limits healthcare, educational, and employment opportunities that are essential for consumer welfare and America's economic growth and global competitiveness. 99

—The FCC, an independent US government agency that is charged with regulating interstate and international communications by radio, television, wire, satellite, and cable.

Jillian Maldonado often feels like she is fighting an impossible battle. The twenty-nine-year-old single mother from New York City is furthering her education by taking classes at the Mid-Manhattan Adult Learning Center while trying to support herself and her nine-year-old son by selling Avon cosmetics. Each day when classes end, Maldonado takes the subway back to her apartment, fixes dinner for her son, and helps him with his homework. Then, because she has customer orders to

50

submit, papers to write for her medical billing class, and online assignments to complete, she walks with her son three blocks to the library to use a computer. Maldonado knows that life would be easier if she could do her online work at home, but she cannot afford a computer or the monthly cost of broadband service. "It's just so exhausting because I use the Internet all the time," she says. "I'm always back and forth to the library. Some days I feel completely defeated."[40]

Libraries Being Stretched

Like Maldonado, millions of people depend on libraries as their only means of accessing the Internet. Libraries provide a service that is invaluable, giving patrons without broadband at home an opportunity to search for jobs, do research, complete projects for school or work, send and receive e-mail, submit online college and job applications, and perform innumerable other tasks. Says Julius Genachowski: "During the day, libraries have become job centers and librarians career counselors—and after school a place where many students go to do homework online. Last year, more than 30 million Americans used library connections to seek and apply for jobs, and 12 million children used them to do homework. Millions of others are using library connections for health information."[41]

Because so many people depend on libraries for computers with Internet access, the American Library Association (ALA) refers to the institutions as a "'toll-free' bridge over the digital divide."[42] The group says that virtually all libraries throughout the United States have broadband-connected computers for public use, with nearly 90 percent pro-

> " With the growing number of people needing high-speed Internet, the budgets and capabilities of libraries throughout the United States are being strained. "

viding technology training to patrons who need it. Yet with the growing number of people needing high-speed Internet, the budgets and capabilities of libraries throughout the United States are being strained. Federal and state funding has been reduced for many libraries, which means they

> **Studies of Internet connectivity have consistently ranked India as lowest among the four BRIC nations, which include Brazil, Russia, India, and China.**

have less money to pay for services that are in ever-greater demand. According to the ALA, 2011 was a particularly bad year for urban libraries, but those in rural areas suffered as well. For a study published in June 2011, seventeen library systems reported the closure of public libraries in their states during the past twelve months, and thirteen had closed the previous year.

The combination of reduced funding and growing demand for services is making it difficult for libraries to accommodate patrons' needs. The June 2011 ALA report showed that in the past year, over 75 percent of libraries had an insufficient number of public computers to accommodate patron needs, and about 45 percent reported that their Internet connection speeds were too slow some or all of the time. Says one library director: "Keeping up with technology is like changing a tire on a moving vehicle. The challenge is not becoming road kill."[43]

Those Left Behind

The digital divide is much more serious a problem in developing nations than in the United States and other industrialized countries. In India, for example, less than 30 percent of citizens have access to the Internet, and those who do are the wealthier and more highly educated classes of society. Says Suneet Singh Tuli, who is the founder and CEO of the web access provider DataWind: "There are hundreds of millions of people in India who do not have access to the Internet. This deprives them of reaping the benefits of [information and communication technology], leading to a serious 'Digital Divide' between those who are participating in the Information Technology revolution and those who are not."[44]

According to Tuli, studies of Internet connectivity have consistently ranked India as lowest among the four BRIC nations, which include Brazil, Russia, India, and China. These countries are often categorized together because they represent large, emerging market economies and are expected to contribute significantly to the growth of a global gross domestic product. Yet even though India is Asia's third-largest economy, says Tuli, it is the only BRIC country to be classified as an "extreme risk," meaning that India's population suffers from a severe lack of digital inclusion. Tuli adds that the most serious digital divide is found in India's rural areas, where only 1.2 percent of people have Internet access. "This is a problem that seems to have always been present in societies," he says. "Given the progress that technology is capable of, these so-called have-nots are in danger of falling even further behind than those that have the technology and the technological knowledge that goes along with it."[45]

Challenges for Kids

Education has been affected by the digital divide in numerous ways. For instance, many students who live in rural areas of the United States have no way to use the Internet outside of school. Says Genachowski: "Without broadband at home, students can't do online homework assignments that teach them 21st century skills, and their parents and teachers can't take advantage of great tools to communicate and help kids succeed."[46] The word *succeed* is key because, according to the FCC, students with a computer and broadband at home have a higher likelihood of graduating from high school than students who do not have home access to high-speed Internet.

One rural area of the United States where few students have broadband connections at home is Ava, Missouri, a small, rural town nestled in the Ozark Mountains. While kids are at school, they can work in computer labs, have access to notebook computers and iPads, and are able to use high-tech production equipment and editing software to produce multimedia projects. School, however, is the only place where they can access high-speed Internet. Says Brian Wilson, the district's superintendent of schools: "When they're here at school we do

> " Even though the US government strongly advocates the digitizing of health records, doing so is not possible for many health-care providers because of the enormous cost. "

our very, very best to service them and to provide them [with technology]. But when they go home, dial-up is just not the same Internet. You just cannot work on some of the same projects at home."[47]

As difficult as it can be for American students not having broadband at home, they are fortunate to be able to use computers with high-speed Internet connections at their schools. This is not the case with young people from many developing countries, where technology in schools is rare to nonexistent. One teacher who observed this firsthand is Vicky Columba (not her real name), who taught migrant children at a boarding school located on the border of Thailand and Myanmar. The classes were overcrowded due to a shortage of classrooms and teachers, and some days the school had no water, but Columba says it was "full of students literally starving to learn. They were fully aware of the potential of education: it could give them access to a better life than the one they had due to the difficult situation in their country." Yet the children were living examples of the digital divide because they had no access to technology. According to Columba, the school had an "ancient computer laboratory" but it "suffered from flooding and represented a hazard as one could get electric shocks from the computers."[48]

Lost Health-Care Advantages

In its March 2010 *National Broadband Plan*, the FCC stressed that high-speed Internet could make major differences in America's health care by improving quality and lowering costs. The agency also stated that if all patients' records were converted to digital format and put online, it would result in savings of $371 billion over fifteen years for US hospitals and $142 billion for physician practices due to safety and efficiency gains. The actual savings, according to the FCC, could be even greater, as the report authors write: "Potential savings from preventing disease and better managing chronic conditions could double these estimates."[49] Yet even though the US government strongly advocates the digitizing of health records, doing so is not possible for many health-care providers because of the enormous cost.

This is becoming an issue of concern among many health-care advocates, who fear that disparities among providers who can and cannot pay for electronic medical records will widen the digital divide even further. Says Ruth Perot, who is head of the National Health IT Collaborative for the Underserved: "On the one hand the potential for IT [information technology] helping is enormous. The flip side is, if it's available in communities that are doing better than others . . . it doesn't take a rocket scientist to see that gaps are going to increase."[50] To examine the problem, the Kaiser Family Foundation conducted a study and published the results in January 2011. One finding was that medical practices primarily serving low-income patients were the least likely to adopt electronic medical records because they simply did not have the money to do so.

> **Of all the people in the United States who are affected by the digital divide, none have been harder hit than tribal populations.**

One such practice is the Ethio American Health Center, which was established in Washington, DC, to serve the large immigrant population from Ethiopia. The center offers specialized care to patients but cannot pay the tens of thousands of dollars it would cost to move from paper files to digitized records. The center's founder and administrator, Dawit Gizaw, would very much like to have an electronic health system so he could better connect patients with specialists and/or other medical facilities they may need. He invited a company to come to the facility and give a demonstration, but he has not been able to raise any funds or secure grants to cover the cost of the system the company proposed. "It would be great," says Gizaw, "but we can't afford it."[51]

Native American Isolation

Of all the people in the United States who are affected by the digital divide, none have been harder hit than tribal populations. Only an estimated 10 percent of homes on tribal lands have high-speed Internet access—lower than some developing countries. The Native Americans who live in these areas already feel isolated because their reservations are located on remote lands, and many have no telephones or electricity. Feeling left out of the digital revolution deepens their sense of isolation, as journalist Gerry Smith writes: "Without reliable access to the Internet, many Native Americans find themselves increasingly isolated, missing out on opportunities to secure jobs, gain degrees through online classes, reach health care practitioners, and even preserve native languages and rituals with new applications that exploit the advantages of the web."[52]

Sonny Clark is a member of the Navajo tribe and lives on remote tribal lands in Crystal, New Mexico. The only way he can use his cell phone is to drive 5 miles (8.05km) up the side of a mountain, where he can get a signal. In order to use the Internet, which is how he keeps in touch with his children living in other states, he must drive to a town 30 miles (48.28km) away. "I'm in no man's land,"[53] says Clark.

Twenty-one-year-old Raleigh Silversmith, also a Navajo, lives in Window Rock, Arizona, and attends New Mexico State University. Like many other young Native Americans, Silversmith is frustrated by the lack of technology on tribal lands and often feels that the town where he lives is going nowhere. So he has decided to leave and has no plans to return to the reservation. "I can't stay here for 10 years hoping that technology will finally come to the reservation," says Silversmith. "For a lot of the younger people here, the motivation is, 'I want to get out of here so I can experience what the rest of the world has.'"[54]

People Are Hurting

The negative effects of the digital divide are numerous for people throughout the world. Without the availability of broadband in their homes, millions depend on libraries, which are strained by shrinking budgets and burgeoning demand. Issues range from students who are slipping behind because technology is not available to them, to the struggles of people on tribal lands who feel isolated from the digital age. Because of growing awareness of the digital divide, these and other problems have been identified—but whether they can be resolved is a matter of uncertainty.

What Are the Consequences of the Digital Divide?

66 Available evidence supports the notion that broadband can create significant economic benefits for those who adopt it. In a global economy and the huge market it represents, this advantage could make the difference between those who succeed and those who do not. 99

—National Telecommunications and Information Administration, *Digital Nation: Expanding Internet Usage*, February 2011. www.ntia.doc.gov.

An agency of the Commerce Department, the NTIA is responsible for advising the president on telecommunications and information policy issues.

66 National challenges like the U.S. broadband adoption rate, reflect individual American citizens' capacity to employ 21st century vehicles of economic mobility such as information and communications technology. Without full participation we jeopardize our competitiveness as a nation. 99

—Minority Business & Economic Report, "The Digital Divide and Its Impact on Our Economy," December 23, 2011. http://nprchamber.org.

The Minority Business & Economic Report promotes economic freedom and entrepreneurship for Puerto Ricans, Hispanics, women, and other minorities.

* Editor's Note: While the definition of a primary source can be narrowly or broadly defined, for the purposes of Compact Research, a primary source consists of: 1) results of original research presented by an organization or researcher; 2) eyewitness accounts of events, personal experience, or work experience; 3) first-person editorials offering pundits' opinions; 4) government officials presenting political plans and/or policies; 5) representatives of organizations presenting testimony or policy.

> ❝Millions are still offline completely, while others can afford only connections over their phone lines or via wireless smartphones. They can thus expect even lower-quality health services, career opportunities, education and entertainment options than they already receive.❞

—Susan P. Crawford, "The New Digital Divide," *New York Times*, December 3, 2011. www.nytimes.com.

Crawford is a professor at the Benjamin N. Cardozo School of Law and former White House special assistant for science, technology, and innovation policy.

> ❝Whether we're talking about jobs, education, or health care, in this day and age, getting online is a necessity, not a convenience. We can't afford to have a third of the country frozen out of the broadband economy.❞

—Julius Genachowski, "Remarks on Broadband Adoption," Federal Communications Commission, November 9, 2011. http://transition.fcc.gov.

Genachowski is chair of the FCC.

> ❝Broadband deployment and adoption in rural America must increase at a faster rate in order to reverse the trend of rural flight.❞

—Mark Bahnson, "Formulation of the 2012 Farm Bill: Rural Development Programs," testimony, House Committee on Agriculture, April 25, 2012. http://agriculture.house.gov.

Bahnson is CEO and general manager of Bloomingdale Communications in Bloomingdale, Michigan.

> ❝People who are living with chronic disease or disability are likely, if they have internet access, to be highly interested in online health information. For those two groups, it is their lack of access to the Internet which holds them back from parity with people who report no chronic conditions.❞

—Susannah Fox, "Health Topics," Pew Internet & American Life Project, February 1, 2011. http://pewinternet.org.

Fox is Pew's associate director for digital strategy.

66 With broadband connectivity, farmers can instantly access accurate, up-to-the-minute weather information and plan accordingly. They can download software updates for automated farm equipment. Should their equipment break down, farmers can send a photo of the broken part to an equipment dealer anywhere in the world, minimizing both repair cost and downtime. 99

—Jesse Ward, "The Smart Rural Community," National Telecommunications Cooperative Association (NTCA), April 2012. www.ntca.org.

Ward is a policy analyst with the NTCA.

66 The 'digital divide' is real and consequential for those communities who cannot attract businesses for lack of Internet infrastructure. 99

—Diane Russell, "Transforming Rural Economies: Bridging the Digital Divide," *Huffington Post*, August 24, 2011. www.huffingtonpost.com.

Russell is a state representative in the Maine House of Representatives.

What Are the Consequences
of the Digital Divide?

- According to the FCC, students with a computer and broadband at home have graduation rates that are **six to eight percentage points higher** than students who do not have home access to high-speed Internet.

- A 2012 report by the World Economic Forum states that some of the poorest countries in **Asia, including Nepal, Tajikistan, and Pakistan**, have some of the lowest broadband penetration rates in the world.

- According to a May 2012 report by the technology organization Connected Nation, businesses that use broadband report median annual revenues that are approximately **$300,000** higher than businesses that do not use broadband.

- According to a 2012 World Economic Forum report, only **13 percent** of individuals in sub-Saharan Africa use the Internet, **8 percent** of households own a computer, and less than **4 percent** have home Internet.

- In an August 2010 survey by the Pew Internet & American Life Project, **34 percent** of Americans considered it a major disadvantage that they cannot access health-related information because of not having broadband in the home.

Perceptions About Lack of Broadband

In a 2010 survey by Pew Research Center's Internet & American Life Project, participants were asked for their opinions about the disadvantages for people who did not have access to high-speed Internet service at home. Most respondents thought that not having access to job and career opportunities was the biggest disadvantage, whereas keeping up with news and information was perceived to be the least important.

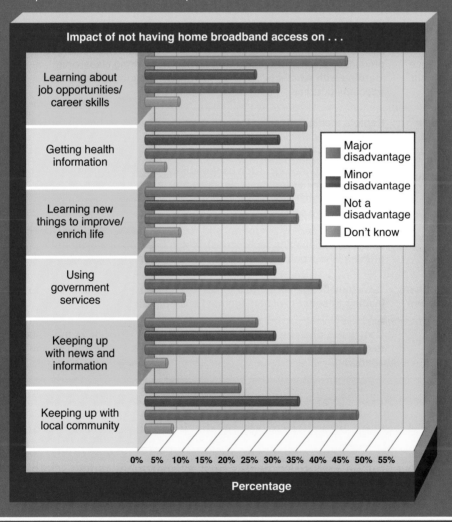

Impact of not having home broadband access on . . .

Source: Aaron Smith, *Home Broadband 2010*, Pew Research Center's Internet & American Life Project, August 11, 2010. http://pewinternet.org.

Lost Opportunities for Rural Residents

The Internet offers innumerable benefits to those who can access it from home. This can be especially beneficial for people living in rural areas far from top-notch schools, first-rate health care, and cutting edge government services. Yet many rural residents cannot take advantage of the benefits because high-speed Internet is not available in their area.

Advantages for rural areas with broadband access	
Distance learning	Schools offer courses online to people who would not be able to physically attend classes as well as supplementing classroom learning with advanced placement, foreign language, and other specialty courses.
Health care	Remote medical diagnostics and monitoring enables quicker, more economically efficient access to specialists.
Agricultural advances	Advanced technology, such as the ability to monitor commodity prices or weather forecasts, enables efficient crop management, leading to higher yields and less waste.
Public safety	Officers can deploy personnel and resources more effectively (such as using 3-D imaging techniques), which frees up deployment of officers who would otherwise be required to remain on-scene.
Government business	Government agencies can interact with citizens with greater ease, leading to better civil management and administration.
Public utilities	Gas, water, and electricity companies can offer consumers the ability to control usage, increase efficiencies, and preserve resources and spending.

Source: Jesse Ward. *The Smart Rural Community*, National Telecommunications Cooperative Association, April 2012.

- According to a 2010 study by the Internet Innovation Alliance, people without broadband access lose out on savings of nearly **$8,000** per year on essential expenses such as apartment rentals, clothing, gasoline, and food.

- A 2011 study by the American Library Association found that **70 percent** of libraries reported increased use of public access computers, but **76 percent** reported an insufficient number of computers to meet demand.

No Broadband Means Lost Savings Opportunities

A 2011 report by the Internet Innovation Alliance concluded that millions of Americans who lack broadband connections in their homes miss out on savings available through online transactions. Consumers with broadband Internet at home can save nearly $8,000 per year on everything from entertainment to food and apparel through online research, purchases, and other steps that save time and money.

Areas of saving due to home broadband Internet		
Category	Average spent per year	Average savings due to broadband
Entertainment	$5,009	$2,444.39
Travel	$7,677	$1,535.40
Housing	$12,963	$1,270.37
Food	$3,624	$942.24
Apparel	$1,700	$542.70
Automotive	$29,217*	$438.26**
Newspapers	$218.87	$195.19
Gasoline	$2,132.96	$132.03
Nonprescription drugs	$390.90	$117.27

*One-time spending on vehicle purchase
**One-time savings on vehicle purchase

Source: Internet Innovation Alliance, "Access to Broadband Internet: Top Ten Areas of Saving 2011," October 12, 2011. http://internetinnovation.org.

- According to a 2012 report by the World Economic Forum, in at least **34 countries** the cost of broadband is higher than the average annual family income.

- A May 2011 report by the FCC states that as many as **80 percent** of schools and libraries funded by the US government's E-rate Technical Assistance Program have Internet service that does not meet their needs, which has a negative impact on learning.

Can the Digital Divide Be Bridged?

66This isn't just about faster Internet or fewer dropped calls. It's about connecting every part of America to the digital age.99

—Barack Obama, forty-fourth president of the United States.

66Like electricity and telephone, broadband has become integral to how people conduct their everyday affairs. It seems only fair, then, to take steps to include everyone.99

—John B. Horrigan, vice president of policy research at TechNet, a network of CEOs that promotes the growth of technology industries.

The Eastern Cape region of South Africa has some of the highest rates of tuberculosis and HIV infection in the world. Doctors are in short supply, so providing adequate health care to large numbers of people, especially those with serious diseases, is a challenging task that often falls on nurses. They would benefit immensely from being able to use the Internet in their work, but connections are rare in this poverty-stricken region: Less than 11 percent of the population has Internet access, and only a fraction of those are connected to broadband. If nurses were able to get online, they could research rare and complex medical cases, keep abreast of the latest updates on epidemics, and obtain information in real time for evaluation of their patients. Thanks to a program called the Mobile Health Information System Project, all these tasks and more are now possible.

The program was implemented in November 2010 by the wireless technology developer Qualcomm, whose Wireless Reach initiative provides broadband access to underserved countries throughout the world. Nurses at a hospital complex in the South African city of Port Elizabeth were given smartphones that were preloaded with an extensive library of resources. By using the devices, nurses are able to expand and update their medical knowledge, to more effectively diagnose and treat patients, and to provide patients with accurate health-care information. One of the nurses in the program, Rochelle Gelandt, says that the smartphone has been invaluable to her. "I have been using it on a daily basis," she says, "the device as well as the mobile library on it. I love that I can access health information at the point of care, as I do not always have the time to go to the library. The device is loaded with so much relevant and interesting content that it is hard not to want to read more."[55]

Meeting a Critical Need in China

Health-care workers in China also face challenges because of the lack of Internet technology, and a smartphone program in that country helped bridge the gap. Cardiovascular disease is the leading cause of death in China. To help prevent the disease and provide better care to patients who suffer from it, Qualcomm initiated the Wireless Heart Health Project in the Chinese provinces of Shandong, Anhui, and Sichuan, and the municipality of Chongqing.

Community health clinics in underserved areas of China were furnished with broadband-connected workstations, and medical providers received smartphones with built-in electrocardiogram sensors. Patients hold the devices in their hands for thirty seconds so heart data can be collected, and providers then send the data to cardiac specialists who staff twenty-four-hour call centers

> " Since its implementation, the Wireless Heart Health Project has made a remarkable difference in providing Chinese patients with quality care. "

in the city of Beijing. For simple cases, physicians in the call center can analyze the data and then provide real-time feedback via a text message or phone call, while patients with more complex cases can be referred to hospitals for further testing or to receive treatment.

Since its implementation, the Wireless Heart Health Project has made a remarkable difference in providing Chinese patients with quality care. In a chapter of the World Economic Forum's 2012 *Global Information Technology Report*, the authors write: "This project demonstrates how . . . mobile broadband can extend the reach of specialized physicians into underserved areas and enable community health clinics to treat more patients effectively."[56]

Reaching Out to Native Americans

In the United States addressing the technology needs of Native Americans is a high priority for the US government. Says Anthony G. Wilhelm, director of the Broadband Technology Opportunities Program: "Too many Native American communities are on the wrong side of the digital divide, lacking access to broadband Internet service and to the economic, educational, and health care opportunities that it enables."[57] A broadband grant initiative by the NTIA is making it possible for high-speed Internet to be extended to tribal lands, as well as for Native Americans to be trained in how to use computers and the Internet.

One of the NTIA's grants benefited the Navajo Nation, which is the largest tribal reservation in the United States and home to approximately 170,000 Native Americans. The Navajo Tribal Utility Authority, which provides utility services to the Navaho Nation, is constructing broadband infrastructure that will eventually cover 15,000 square

> As part of the effort to eradicate the digital divide among Native American communities and to encourage investment in broadband infrastructure, the federal government is providing grants and low-interest loans to telecommunications companies that serve tribal lands.

miles (38,850 sq. km) in Arizona, Utah, and New Mexico. When it is completed, thirty thousand households, one thousand businesses, and eleven hundred institutions in the Navaho Nation will have access to high-speed Internet for the first time. Another project in the works is the construction of forty-nine broadband-connected Chapter Houses, which will serve as community centers for the Navajo population. This, according to Wilhelm, will "pave the way to bring telemedicine services, such as remote diagnostics and patient consultations, to this rural population."[58]

> " Those who are leading the charge to bridge the digital divide are convinced that expanding digital literacy is a critical part of the effort. "

As part of the effort to eradicate the digital divide among Native American communities and to encourage investment in broadband infrastructure, the federal government is providing grants and low-interest loans to telecommunications companies that serve tribal lands. One of these providers, Sacred Wind Communications, is a small, privately owned company based in Albuquerque, New Mexico, that furnishes telephone and Internet services to Navaho Nation households. By obtaining federal loans, Sacred Wind has been able to expand its service area to thousands of additional Native Americans, one of whom is seventy-three-year-old Everett Baldwin. A Navaho medicine man, Baldwin tried for sixteen years to get telephone service at his remote home on top of a small mountain but was unsuccessful. Then in 2010 Sacred Wind constructed a tower on his property, which gave him not only telephone service but also high-speed Internet. Baldwin handcrafts ceremonial teepees and is now able to sell his creations online for $800 each to customers as far away as Australia and Japan. This has made a major difference in his life, as he explains: "To be able to afford Internet makes me feel like a millionaire."[59]

Zeroing in on Digital Literacy

As valuable as it is for people to understand technology and make use of it, research has shown that millions of individuals still do not use the Internet. According to the NTIA's 2011 *Digital Nation* report, the most common reason given for this is lack of interest: Nonusers do not perceive being online as something that is important or that has value for them. Many experts attribute this to having little or no knowledge of technology, along with a lack of understanding of how much broadband could benefit their lives. In other words, these users lack what is known as digital literacy, meaning the skills to use a computer and navigate the Internet. A paper by the Communications Workers of America describes how essential digital literacy is in today's information age:

> Digitally literate Americans are more attractive to prospective employers, and businesses comfortable with digital technology are more economically competitive. Tech-savvy students use high speed Internet to improve their academic performance and prepare for future jobs. Broadband enables people familiar with teleconferencing and online social networks to strengthen their ties with faraway friends and family. Fundamentally, high speed Internet is a tool with endless potential, and only the digitally literate have the skills to harness it effectively.[60]

Those who are leading the charge to bridge the digital divide are convinced that expanding digital literacy is a critical part of the effort. In October 2011 Julius Genachowski announced the implementation of Connect 2 Compete, which is a nationwide initiative to increase digital literacy and to promote adoption of high-speed Internet. The program is a collaborative partnership between government agencies, community leaders, the private sector, nonprofit organizations such as United Way Worldwide, and charitable foundations. One of the companies involved in the effort is retailer Best Buy, which has committed twenty thousand of its Geek Squad agents to provide digital literacy training in cities throughout the United States, as well as to work with community groups to train people how to teach digital literacy to others. Says Genachowski: "We're building tremendous momentum in our efforts to

> " A number of charitable organizations are making it a priority to help bridge the digital divide. "

connect every American and seize the benefits of broadband."[61]

When Genachowski announced that tackling digital literacy was a national priority, he challenged Internet providers to do their part to make the goal a reality, and they accepted the challenge. Thirteen ISPs initiated an innovative program that allows low-income families in the United States to receive broadband service for just $9.95 per month. Those who do not have computers can purchase a notebook for the reduced price of $150. One of these providers was Cox Communications, which is among the largest ISPs in the United States. In preparation for its nationwide launch, Cox initiated a pilot program in California's San Diego County in May 2012. According to county officials, nearly 30 percent of the county's 495,000 public school students do not have computers or Internet connections at home, and an estimated thirteen thousand families meet the criteria for the reduced-fee Internet program. Says elementary principal Ginger Van Zant: "I think it just opens up the world for families that don't have that kind of access."[62]

Foundations Form Bridges

A number of charitable organizations are making it a priority to help bridge the digital divide. One is the Bill & Melinda Gates Foundation, which was started by Microsoft founder Bill Gates. In November 2011 the foundation donated $30 million, along with $3.6 million in software, toward an initiative that provides basic computer skills and Internet training to nearly eight hundred thousand people living in rural areas of Vietnam. Over the course of five years, computers with broadband connections will be installed at nearly two thousand public libraries in forty Vietnamese provinces, and library staff will be trained to support the technology needs of patrons. Says Deborah Jacobs, the foundation's Global Libraries Initiative director: "We have seen how access to information and technology can make a powerful difference to the lives of people across Vietnam. As we expand the project, our success will depend upon our collective engagement, as we invest and learn together. It is only with the continued commitment of the Vietnamese Government and other partners that we can bring about sustainable change."[63]

Another charitable organization that is committed to bridging the digital divide is the Knight Foundation. One of its programs targeted Detroit, Michigan, a city where poverty is rampant and less than 40 percent of households have broadband access. A project called the Detroit Connected Community Initiative, which was implemented in 2009, focused on three of the city's poorest neighborhoods. The Foundation awarded over $800,000 to develop a broadband network, to purchase computers for residents, and to form a digital literacy training program, in which participants would learn how to use web browsers, upload documents such as resumes to the Internet, and use search engines to find information.

One Detroit resident who benefited from the program is fifty-three-year-old Jean Caldwell, who knew very little about computer technology before enrolling in digital literacy classes. Initially, her goal was to gain some basic computer skills and also to better understand what her grandson was doing in school. After she graduated from the class, however, she decided that she might be able to achieve something that had been on her mind for many years: earning her high school diploma. Caldwell was amazed at all that she learned through the training—and how much she had been missing by not understanding how to use the Internet. "Everything you want is in there, on the Internet," she says. "You just gotta know how to go find it."[64]

A Bridge to Somewhere

The digital divide is a formidable problem throughout the world—but it is not a problem that is being ignored. Collaborative efforts by government agencies, charitable foundations, major corporations, nonprofit groups, and private individuals are making a positive difference in narrowing the gap between those who are fortunate enough to have access to Internet technology and those who are not. This is by no means a simple undertaking, nor is it one that can erase the problem overnight. But as efforts continue and more people are reached, the term *digital divide* may someday be used only in reference to the past.

Primary Source Quotes*

Can the Digital Divide Be Bridged?

❝Equalizing access to broadband is a civil rights matter of the greatest importance.❞

—David Honig, "More Wireless Broadband Is What Consumers Want, U.S. Needs to Close the Digital Divide," *Huffington Post*, January 3, 2012. www.huffingtonpost.com.

Honig is cofounder of the Minority Media and Telecommunications Council.

❝Technology is an enabler of rights, not a right itself.❞

—Vinton G. Cerf, "Internet Access Is Not a Human Right," *New York Times*, January 4, 2012. www.nytimes.com.

Cerf, a computer scientist, is recognized as one of the fathers of the Internet and is a vice president at Google.

❝Getting all Americans online is key to our nation's economic success.❞

—Julius Genachowski, "Remarks on Broadband Adoption," Federal Communications Commission, November 9, 2011. http://transition.fcc.gov.

Genachowski is chair of the FCC.

* Editor's Note: While the definition of a primary source can be narrowly or broadly defined, for the purposes of Compact Research, a primary source consists of: 1) results of original research presented by an organization or researcher; 2) eyewitness accounts of events, personal experience, or work experience; 3) first-person editorials offering pundits' opinions; 4) government officials presenting political plans and/or policies; 5) representatives of organizations presenting testimony or policy.

66 **People with disabilities should have the same choice in everyday telecommunications as other people—in access, quality, and price.** 99

—World Health Organization, *World Report on Disability*, June 9, 2011.
http://whqlibdoc.who.int/publications/2009/9789241598682_eng.pdf

The World Health Organization is the directing and coordinating authority for health within the United Nations system.

66 **Congress and many other U.S. institutions have acknowledged that leaving rural America in its current broadband adoption position is simply unacceptable.** 99

—James N. Barnes, "Strengthening Rural America's Position in the Global Broadband Adoption Race," *Choices*, 4th Quarter 2010. www.choicesmagazine.org.

Barnes is an associate professor at Louisiana State University and director of the Louisiana Center for Rural Initiatives.

66 **Is there a basis for society to promote the deployment and adoption of broadband Internet? Although research is in its early stages, the available evidence supports the notion that broadband can create significant economic benefits.** 99

—National Telecommunications and Information Administration, *Digital Nation: Expanding Internet Usage*, February 2011. www.ntia.doc.gov.

An agency of the Commerce Department, the NTIA is responsible for advising the president on telecommunications and information policy issues.

66 **Closing the 'digital divide'—the gap between society's tech-enabled haves and have-nots—hinges on enhancing the quality and breadth of consumer access to digital and information technology in areas such as education, employment, health care, news and entertainment.** 99

—Brookings Institution, "Bridging the Digital Divide: Spectrum Policy, Program Diversity and Consumer Rights," May 5, 2011. www.brookings.edu.

The Brookings Institution is a public policy organization based in Washington, DC.

66 As more and more commerce, government services, and education move over broadband, it will only become more important to provide this service to rural areas to bolster economic activity that will be necessary to attract and retain more Americans. 99

—Mark Bahnson, "Formulation of the 2012 Farm Bill: Rural Development Programs," testimony, House Committee on Agriculture, April 25, 2012. http://agriculture.house.gov.

Bahnson is CEO and general manager of Bloomingdale Communications in Bloomingdale, Michigan.

66 Major steps need to be taken to bridge the speed and price disparities separating the U.S. from other industrialized countries. 99

—James Losey and Chiehyu Li, *Price of the Pipe: Comparing the Price of Broadband Services Around the Globe*. New America Foundation, April 2010. http://newamerica.net.

Losey is a policy analyst with the New America Foundation's Open Technology Institute, and Li is a program associate with the same group.

Facts and Illustrations

Can the Digital Divide Be Bridged?

- According to a February 2011 report by Euromonitor International, increased broadband connectivity in developing nations could help improve education and **literacy levels**, which are far below those of industrialized countries.

- To help bridge the digital divide in countries such as Sri Lanka and India, ISPs are starting to offer connections for as low as **two dollars per month**.

- According to FCC chair Julius Genachowski, research has shown that closing the broadband adoption gap would create **$32 billion** in annual economic value.

- The FCC states that **18 million** Americans living in unserved rural areas will receive access to broadband over the next decade.

- The Australian government has invested **$43 billion** in its National Broadband Network project, with the goal of extending 100 Mbps broadband to every home and business in the country.

- In January 2011 the Obama administration announced its **National Wireless Initiative**, whose goal is to ensure that at least **98 percent** of Americans have access to high-speed wireless Internet service within five years.

An Aggressive Goal to Get Americans Connected

Based on a 2009 congressional mandate, the Federal Communications Commission developed a national broadband plan. The agency hopes this plan will go a long way toward bridging the digital divide. Here are the long-term goals for the plan.

Goal #1	At least 100 million US homes should have affordable access to actual download speeds of at least 100 megabits per second and actual upload speeds of at least 50 megabits per second.
Goal #2	The United States should lead the world in mobile innovation, with the fastest and most extensive wireless networks of any nation.
Goal #3	Every American should have affordable access to robust broadband service and the means and skills to subscribe if they so choose.
Goal #4	Every American community should have affordable access to at least 1 gigabit per second broadband service to anchor institutions such as schools, hospitals, and government buildings.
Goal #5	To ensure the safety of the American people, every first responder should have access to a nationwide, wireless, interoperable broadband public safety network.
Goal #6	To ensure that America leads in the clean energy economy, Americans should be able to use broadband to track and manage their real-time energy consumption

Source: Federal Communications Commission, *Connecting America: The National Broadband Plan*, March 2010. http://download.broadband.gov.

- According to a February 2011 report by Euromonitor International, greater broadband connectivity and usage in developing countries could help raise the skills of workers, making people more **employable and better able to earn higher incomes.**

- According to the FCC, **five hundred thousand new jobs** will be created as a direct result of new broadband deployment in rural areas of the United States.

Digital Divide Narrowing in Developing Countries

Developing countries still lag behind developed nations in Internet use, but according to the International Telecommunications Union that trend is starting to change. The group notes that over the past five years developing countries have made important strides in catching up to the rest of the world. These charts show progress between 2006 and 2011.

Share of Internet users in the global population

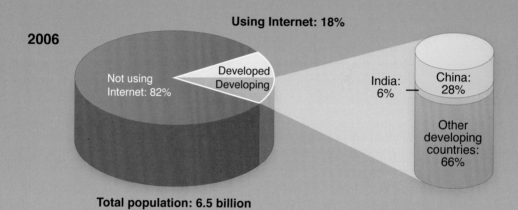

2006

Using Internet: 18%

Not using Internet: 82%

Developed
Developing

India: 6%
China: 28%

Other developing countries: 66%

Total population: 6.5 billion

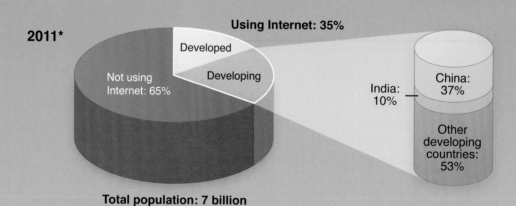

2011*

Using Internet: 35%

Developed

Not using Internet: 65%

Developing

India: 10%
China: 37%

Other developing countries: 53%

Total population: 7 billion

Note: *2011 figures are estimates.

Source: International Telecommunications Union, *ICT Facts and Figures*, 2011. www.itu.int.

- In October 2009 Finland became the first country in the world to declare that broadband Internet access is a **legal right** for all citizens.

- According to FCC chair Julius Genachowski, the private sector invested over **$60 billion** in 2010 to expand broadband capacity, increase speeds on existing networks, and roll out next-generation mobile services.

- As part of its 2010 *National Broadband Plan*, the FCC's goal is for at least **100 million** US homes to have affordable access to 100 Mbps broadband within a decade.

Key People and Advocacy Groups

V.A. Shiva Ayyadurai: The inventor of electronic mail who holds the copyright for EMAIL, a system he began building in 1978 when he was only fourteen years old.

Tim Berners-Lee: A computer expert from England who created the World Wide Web and launched it in 1991.

Vinton G. Cerf: A computer scientist who is recognized as the father of the Internet and now serves as vice president and chief Internet evangelist for Google.

Federal Communications Commission (FCC): An independent US government agency that is charged with regulating interstate and international communications by radio, television, wire, satellite, and cable.

Julius Genachowski: Chair of the FCC and a strong advocate for making broadband available to every household in the United States.

International Telecommunications Union (ITU): An agency of the United Nations that specializes in information and communication technologies.

James Katz and Philip Aspden: Researchers from New Jersey who in 1995 conducted one of the first demographic surveys on Internet use, thus confirming their belief that the digital divide existed.

Lloyd Morrisett: A psychologist, philanthropist, and founder of the Sesame Street Workshop who is credited with coining the term *digital divide* in the 1990s.

National Telecommunications and Information Administration (NTIA): An agency of the US Commerce Department that is responsible for advising the president on telecommunications and information policy issues.

Organisation for Economic Co-operation and Development (OECD): An organization based in Paris, France, whose mission is to promote policies that will improve the economic and social well-being of people throughout the world and which has prepared extensive reports on the global digital divide.

Chronology

1969
The first test of AR-PANET (Advanced Research Projects Agency Network) is successful, proving that computers can be linked together to communicate with each other; a rudimentary version of the Internet is launched.

1978
V.A. Shiva Ayyadurai, a fourteen-year-old from New Jersey, invents the electronic mail system; later he patents his invention and obtains the copyright for the term *EMAIL*.

1990
British computer expert Tim Berners-Lee finishes development of software, a point-and-click browser, and the world's first web server; the following year he announces the creation on four Internet newsgroups, marking the official launch of the World Wide Web.

1970

1985

1973
The University College of London and Norway's Royal Radar Establishment connect to ARPANET, marking the network's first international connections.

1988
Delegates from 114 countries gather in Melbourne, Australia, to agree to a treaty that privatizes the Internet by insulating it from economic and technical regulation by any government.

1991
The High Performance Computing Act of 1991 is signed into law; it allocates $600 million for high-performance computing and creates the National Research and Education Network.

1994
The National Center for Education Statistics reports that 35 percent of public schools in the United States have Internet access.

1995
The NTIA releases a report that explains how racial minorities, the poor, and people living in rural areas do not have the same access to telephone service and the Internet as wealthier households.

1997

A report titled *Computers and Classrooms: The Status of Technology in U.S. Schools* cites major differences among schools' access to educational technology: Students who attend poor and high-minority schools have less access to this technology than those attending other schools.

2011

The NTIA announces the completion of a national broadband map, which is the first public, searchable nationwide map of broadband Internet availability.

2010

In a poll of over twenty-seven thousand adults worldwide by BBC World Service, nearly 80 percent of participants say that Internet access should be the fundamental right of all people.

2005

The FCC defines telephone DSL broadband as an information service, in line with its 2002 decision about cable modem service.

2000

2010

2002

The FCC classifies cable Internet service as an interstate information service, rather than a telecommunications service, meaning that it is not subject to the same regulations that govern telephone companies.

2009

Finland becomes the first country in the world to declare that broadband Internet access is a legal right for all citizens.

2006

A survey by the Pew Internet & American Life Project finds that 42 percent of Americans have high-speed Internet at home, up from 30 percent in 2005.

2012

The International Telecommunication Union, a United Nations organization, declares its intention to revise the 1988 deregulation treaty and subject the Internet to international regulatory control.

Related Organizations

Center for Digital Inclusion (CDI)

Rio de Janeiro, Brazil
e-mail: contact@cdiglobal.org • website: http://cdiglobal.org

The CDI supports educational programs that are designed to expose low-income communities to new technologies. Its website offers facts about the digital divide, news releases, and information about its digital inclusion programs.

Connected Nation

PO Box 43586
Washington, DC 20010
e-mail: info@connectednation.org • website: www.connectednation.org
phone: (877) 846-7710

Connected Nation facilitates public and private partnerships to increase access to and use of broadband and related technology. Its website offers research about the digital divide, broadband maps, videos, news releases, and a link to the organization's blog and Facebook page.

Federal Communications Commission (FCC)

445 Twelfth St. SW
Washington, DC 20554
phone: (888) 225-5322 • fax: (866) 418-0232
e-mail: fccinfo@fcc.gov • website: www.fcc.gov

The FCC is an independent US government agency that is charged with regulating interstate and international communications by radio, television, wire, satellite, and cable. Its website offers a wealth of information, including national studies, the national broadband map, statistics, and a search engine that produces numerous articles about the digital divide.

International Telecommunications Union (ITU)

Place des Nations
1211 Geneva 20
Switzerland
phone: +41 22 730 5852 • fax: 41 22 730 5853
e-mail: tsbmail@itu.int • website: www.itu.int

The ITU is an agency of the United Nations that specializes in information and communication technologies. Its website features videos, the *ITU News* online magazine, news releases, statistics, and a search engine that produces numerous publications about the digital divide.

National Telecommunications and Information Administration (NTIA)

US Department of Commerce
Herbert C. Hoover Building
1401 Constitution Ave. NW
Washington, DC 20230
phone: (202) 482-2000
website: www.ntia.doc.gov

An agency of the Commerce Department, the NTIA is responsible for advising the president on telecommunications and information policy issues. An extensive array of information about the digital divide is available on its website, including sections on digital literacy, broadband, Internet policy, and the national broadband map.

National Telecommunications Cooperative Association (NTCA)

4121 Wilson Blvd., Suite 1000
Arlington, VA 22203
phone: (703) 351-2000 • fax: (703) 351-2001
e-mail: info@ntca.org • website: www.ntca.org

The NTCA is a nonprofit association that represents over 570 small and rural telephone cooperatives and commercial companies. Its website features an extensive "Tech Knowledge" section, reports on broadband adoption programs, news articles, webcasts, and a search engine that produces many articles about the digital divide.

New America Foundation Open Technology Institute

1899 L St. NW, Suite 400
Washington, DC 20036
phone: (202) 986-2700 • fax: (202) 986-3696
website: http://oti.newamerica.net

The Open Technology Institute is dedicated to Internet freedom and open technology. Its website features news releases, policy papers, podcasts, and a search engine that produces numerous articles about issues related to the digital divide.

Organisation for Economic Co-operation and Development (OECD)

2, rue André Pascal
75775 Paris Cedex 16
France
phone: +33 1 45 24 82 00 • fax: +33 1 45 24 85 00
website: www.oecd.org

The OECD's mission is to promote policies that will improve the economic and social well-being of people throughout the world. Its website features statistics, reports, working papers, news releases, and a search engine that produces publications related to the digital divide.

Pew Internet & American Life Project

1615 L St. NW, Suite 700
Washington, DC 20036
phone: (202) 419-4500 • fax: (202) 419-4505
e-mail: info@ pewinternet.org • website: http://pewinternet.org

The Pew Internet & American Life Project produces reports that explore the social impact of the Internet on families, communities, and populations. Its website offers news releases, a topic section, and a search engine that produces archived surveys and reports.

World Economic Forum

91-93 route de la Capite,
CH-1223 Cologny/Geneva
Switzerland
phone: +41 (0) 22 869 1212 • fax: +41 (0) 22 786 2744
e-mail: contact@weforum.org • website: www.weforum.org

The World Economic Forum is a global community of business, political, intellectual, and other societal leaders who are committed to improving the state of the world. Its website features a wide variety of publications, including the comprehensive *Global Information Technology Report* published in 2012.

For Further Research

Books

Mark Bauerlein, *The Digital Divide: Arguments for and Against Facebook, Google, Texting, and the Age of Social Networking*. New York: Jeremy P. Tarcher/Penguin, 2011.

Shelly Palmer and Mike Raffensperger, *Overcoming the Digital Divide*. Rye Brook, NY: York House, 2011.

Peter B. Seel, *Digital Universe: The Global Telecommunication Revolution*. Malden, MA: Wiley-Blackwell, 2012.

Joseph Straubhaar, Jeremiah Spence, Zeynep Tufekci, and Roberta G. Lentz, eds., *Inequity in the Technopolis: Race, Class, Gender, and the Digital Divide in Austin*. Austin: University of Texas Press, 2012.

Jessamyn C. West, *Without a Net: Librarians Bridging the Digital Divide*. Santa Barbara, CA: Libraries Unlimited, 2011.

Periodicals

Susan P. Crawford, "The New Digital Divide," *New York Times*, December 3, 2011.

Noeleen Heyzer, "Digital Asia-Pacific in the Twenty-First Century: Promises and Perils in the Creation of an Inclusive Knowledge Society," *UN Chronicle*, September 2011.

Lucy Hood, "Smartphones Are Bridging the Digital Divide," *Wall Street Journal*, August 29, 2011.

Cecilia Kang, "Survey of Online Access Finds Digital Divide," *Washington Post*, February 17, 2011.

Barbara Kiviat, "The End of the Racial Digital Divide?," *Time*, July 8, 2010.

Kym McNicholas, "The Fastest Internet Speeds in the World," *Forbes*, January 24, 2011.

Bobby Oerzen, "Battle of the Bands: Why Is the United States Losing the Internet Race?," *Current Science*, a Weekly Reader publication, January 13, 2012.

Kelsey Sheehy, "Rural Students Lost in Connectivity Gap," *U.S. News & World Report*, November 22, 2011.

Patricia Smith, "The Digital Divide," *New York Times Upfront*, May 9, 2011.

Randall Stross, "Cheap, Ultrafast Broadband? Hong Kong Has It," *New York Times*, March 5, 2011.

Deborah M. Todd, "Plenty of Internet Users Cling to Slow Dial-Up Connections," *Pittsburgh Post-Gazette*, March 12, 2012.

Eduardo Ulibarri, "A Strong, UN-Based Digital Bridge," *UN Chronicle*, September 2011.

Internet Sources

John Dunbar, "Wealthy Suburbs Get Best Broadband Deals; D.C., Rural Areas Lag Behind," Investigative Reporting Workshop, February 18, 2011. http://investigativereportingworkshop.org/connected/story/washington-dc-broadband-speed.

John C. Dvorak, "The Absurdity of the Digital Divide," *PC Magazine*, April 5, 2012. www.pcmag.com/article2/0,2817,2402670,00.asp.

Economic and Statistics Administration and National Telecommunications and Information Administration, *Exploring the Digital Nation: Computer and Internet Use at Home*, November 2011. www.ntia.doc.gov/files/ntia/publications/exploring_the_digital_nation_computer_and_internet_use_at_home_11092011.pdf.

David Honig, "More Wireless Broadband Is What Consumers Want, U.S. Needs to Close the Digital Divide," *Huffington Post*, January 3, 2012. www.huffingtonpost.com/david-honig/more-wireless-broadband-i_b_1161068.html.

David Nagel, "Will Smart Phones Eliminate the Digital Divide?," *The Journal*, February 1, 2011. http://thejournal.com/articles/2011/02/01/will-smart-phones-eliminate-the-digital-divide.aspx.

Katia Savchuk, "Massive Digital Divide for Native Americans Is 'a Travesty,'" PBS, May 12, 2011. www.pbs.org/mediashift/2011/05/massive-digital-divide-for-native-americans-is-a-travesty132.html.

Gerry Smith, "Without Internet, Urban Poor Fear Being Left Behind in Information Age," *Huffington Post*, March 1, 2012. www.huffingtonpost.com/2012/03/01/internet-access-digital-age_n_1285423.html.

Source Notes

Overview

1. Quoted in Walter Pacheco, "Many Low-Income Students Struggle with Lack of Internet at Home," *Orlando (FL) Sentinel*, March 18, 2012. http://articles.orlandosentinel.com.

2. Brookings Institution, "Bridging the Digital Divide: Spectrum Policy, Program Diversity and Consumer Rights," May 5, 2011. www.brookings.edu.

3. National Telecommunications and Information Administration, *Digital Nation: Expanding Internet Usage*, February 2011. www.ntia.doc.gov.

4. James N. Barnes, "Strengthening Rural America's Position in the Global Broadband Adoption Race," *Choices*, 4th Quarter 2010. www.choicesmagazine.org.

5. Federal Communications Commission, "Improving Communications Services for Native Nations," March 4, 2011. http://transition.fcc.gov.

6. Federal Communications Commission, "Improving Communications Services for Native Nations."

7. International Telecommunications Union, *The World in 2011: ICT Facts and Figures*, October 25, 2011. www.itu.int.

8. National Telecommunications and Information Administration, *Falling Through the Net: A Survey of the "Have Nots" in Rural and Urban America*, July 1995. www.ntia.doc.gov.

9. Aaron Smith, *Home Broadband 2010*, Pew Internet & American Life Project, August 11, 2010. http://pewinternet.org.

10. Julius Genachowski, "Statement of Chairman Julius Genachowski," Federal Communications Commission *Seventh Broadband Progress Report and Order on Reconsideration*, May 20, 2011. http://transition.fcc.gov.

11. Quoted in Nick Pandolfo, "As Some Schools Plunge into Technology, Poor Schools Are Left Behind," *Hechinger Report*, January 24, 2012. http://hechingerreport.org.

12. Julius Genachowski, *Remarks on Broadband Adoption* (before Pew Charitable Trust), Federal Communications Commission, October 12, 2011. http://hraunfoss.fcc.gov.

13. Quoted in Gerry Smith, "Without Internet, Urban Poor Fear Being Left Behind in Digital Age," *Huffington Post*, March 1, 2012. www.huffingtonpost.com.

14. Pamela Lewis Dolan, "New Vital Sign: Degree of Patient's Online Access," AmedNews, February 21, 2011. www.ama-assn.org.

15. Quoted in Alan Mozes, "Digital Divide Opens Up in Patient Use of Online Medical Records," HealthDay, March 30, 2011. http://health.usnews.com.

16. Genachowski, *Remarks on Broadband Adoption* (before Pew Charitable Trusts).

What Is the Digital Divide?

17. James Katz and Philip Aspden, "Motivation for and Barriers to Internet Usage: Results of a National Public Opinion Survey," *Internet Research Journal*, Fall 1997, p. 171.

18. John C. Dvorak, "U.S. Lags in Internet Connectivity Speeds," *PC Magazine*, May 4, 2012. www.pcmag.com.

19. Quoted in Pandolfo, "As Some

Schools Plunge into Technology, Poor Schools Are Left Behind."

20. Quoted in Patricia Smith, "The Digital Divide," *New York Times Upfront*, May 9, 2011, p. 6.

21. Susannah Fox, "Americans Living with Disability and Their Technology Profile," Pew Internet & American Life Project, January 21, 2011. www.pewinternet.org.

22. World Health Organization, *World Report on Disability*, June 9, 2011. http://whqlibdoc.who.int.

23. Darrell M. West, "Ten Facts About Mobile Broadband," Center for Technology Innovation at Brookings," December 8, 2011. www.brookings.edu.

24. Susan P. Crawford, "The New Digital Divide," *New York Times*, December 3, 2011. www.nytimes.com.

25. Crawford, "The New Digital Divide."

26. Genachowski, *Remarks on Broadband Adoption* (before Pew Charitable Trusts).

What Are the Causes of the Digital Divide?

27. Federal Communications Commission, "FCC Classifies Cable Modem Service as 'Information Service,'" March 14, 2002. http://transition.fcc.gov.

28. *Scientific American*, editorial, "Why Broadband Service in the U.S. Is So Awful," October 4, 2010. www.scientificamerican.com.

29. Tom Smith, comment on *Scientific American*, "Why Broadband Service in the U.S. Is So Awful."

30. Smith, comment on *Scientific American*, "Why Broadband Service in the U.S. Is So Awful."

31. Crawford, "The New Digital Divide."

32. Berkman Center for Internet & Society at Harvard University, *Next Generation Connectivity: A Review of Broadband Internet Transitions and Policy from Around the World*, February 2010. http://cyber.law.harvard.edu.

33. James Losey and Chichyu Li, "Price of the Pipe: Comparing the Price of Broadband Services Around the Globe," New America Foundation, April 2010. http://newamerica.net.

34. *Scientific American*, "Why Broadband Service in the U.S. Is So Awful."

35. John Dunbar, "Poverty Stretches the Digital Divide," Investigative Reporting Workshop, March 23, 2012. http://investigativereportingworkshop.org.

36. Dunbar, "Poverty Stretches the Digital Divide."

37. Quoted in Dunbar, "Poverty Stretches the Digital Divide."

38. John B. Horrigan, "Broadband Adoption and Use in America," OBI Working Paper Series No. 1, February 2010. http://online.wsj.com.

39. Quoted in Deborah M. Todd, "Plenty of Internet Users Cling to Slow Dial-Up Connections," *Pittsburgh Post-Gazette*, March 12, 2012. www.post-gazette.com.

What Are the Consequences of the Digital Divide?

40. Quoted in Smith, "Without Internet, Urban Poor Fear Being Left Behind in Digital Age."

41. Genachowski, *Remarks on Broadband Adoption* (before Pew Charitable Trusts).

42. American Library Association, "Public Library Funding & Technology Access Study 2010-2011: Executive Summary," June 21, 2011. www.ala.org.

43. Quoted in American Library Association, "Reports from the Field," June 21, 2011. www.ala.org.

44. Suneet Singh Tuli, "Bridging the Digital Divide," *Management Compass*, January 2012. www.mediamates.biz.

45. Tuli, "Bridging the Digital Divide."

46. Julius Genachowski, *Remarks on Broadband Adoption* (before the Langley Education Campus), Federal Communications Commission, November 9, 2011. http://hraunfoss.fcc .gov.

47. Quoted in Kelsey Sheehy, "Rural Students Lost in Connectivity Gap," *US News & World Report*, November 22, 2011. www.usnews.com.

48. Vicky Columba, "The Digital Divide: A Tale of Two Schools," UNESCO, January 19, 2012. www.unesco.org.

49. Federal Communications Commission, *Connecting America: The National Broadband Plan*, June 2010. http://download.broadband.gov.

50. Quoted in Emma Schwartz, "Digital Divide Threatens Health Care," Kaiser Health News, January 11, 2011. www.kaiserhealthnews.org.

51. Quoted in Schwartz, "Digital Divide Threatens Health Care."

52. Gerry Smith, "On Tribal Lands, Digital Divide Brings New Form of Isolation," *Huffington Post*, April 23, 2012. www.huffingtonpost.com /2012/04/20/digital-divide-tribal-la nds_n_1403046.html.

53. Quoted in Smith, "On Tribal Lands, Digital Divide Brings New Form of Isolation."

54. Quoted in Smith, "On Tribal Lands, Digital Divide Brings New Form of Isolation."

Can the Digital Divide Be Bridged?

55. Quoted in Qualcomm, "Case Study: Mobile Health Information System: Providing Access to Information for Health Care Workers," October 2011. www.qualcomm.com.

56. William Bold and William Davidson, "Mobile Broadband: Redefining Internet Access and Empowering Individuals," in *The Global Information Technology Report 2012*, Soumitra Dutta and Beñat Bilbao-Osorio, eds. World Economic Forum, 2012. www3.weforum.org.

57. Anthony G. Wilhelm, "Closing the Digital Divide: Focus on Native American Communities," National Telecommunications and Information Administration, December 14, 2011. www.ntia.doc.gov.

58. Wilhelm, "Closing the Digital Divide."

59. Quoted in Smith, "Without Internet, Urban Poor Fear Being Left Behind in Digital Age."

60. Communications Workers of America, *High Speed Internet and Digital Literacy*. http://files.cwa-union.org.

61. Genachowski, *Remarks on Broadband Adoption* (before the Langley Education Campus).

62. Quoted in Karen Kucher, "San Diego Piloting National Push for Digital Literacy," *San Diego Union-Tribune*, May 11, 2012. www.utsandiego.com.

63. Quoted in Bill & Melinda Gates Foundation, "Vietnam's Public Libraries Offer Improved Access to Information and Technology," November 10, 2011. www.gatesfoundation.org.

64. Quoted in Fara Warner, *Connect Detroit: Lessons from One City's Efforts to Bridge the Digital Divide*, Knight Foundation, 2012. www.knightfound ation.org.

List of Illustrations

Index

Note: page numbers in bold indicate an illustration

About the Author

Peggy J. Parks holds a bachelor of science degree from Aquinas College in Grand Rapids, Michigan, where she graduated magna cum laude. An author who has written over one hundred educational books for children and young adults, Parks lives in Muskegon, Michigan, a town that she says inspires her writing because of its location on the shores of Lake Michigan.